"*We Are Engaged!* is a balm for my broken and lost heart, reminding me of my desperate need for unconditional love in Jesus. Craig does an amazing work of explaining the second of God's best object lessons of all history, the first being the sacrificial system pointing to Jesus's atoning sacrifice. Marriage helps us envision the agape love that he has for us and Craig draws out, from Scripture, the full meaning of this metaphor beautifully."

—**Martin Kohlwey**, Director of Campus Ministry, Lutheran High School, Parker, Colorado

"*We Are Engaged!* fed my imagination and heightened my anticipation for the return of Christ. Through extensive use of Scripture, Craig has dealt candidly with this world's heartache and set Christ as the center of my gaze."

—**Daniel Vanderhyde**, Chaplain, Lutheran High School, Parker, Colorado

"This book covers a view of our salvation that offers more meaning and insight into our state here on earth than I normally think. Sanctification for me has meant only that spiritual cleansing portion of my walk, a journey of self-improvement enabled, powered, and directed by the Holy Spirit. *We Are Engaged!* offers an additional view, the depth and meaning and appreciation of our position as bride-in-waiting. It is perfect for every believer who wants a broader view into sanctification."

—**Walt Keith**, Airline Pilot

"In his book, *We Are Engaged!*, Craig Parrott does a masterful job of using the image of our earthly engagement and preparations for marriage as a framework for our life with Christ both now and in eternity. This book is for anyone who has tried to find fulfillment in the myriad options the world offers only to be left wanting. And for those who are followers of Jesus, it will help refocus their life as a disciple. This book is a breath of fresh air filled with the peace, encouragement, and hope we have in Christ!"

—**Bobby Walston**, Pastor, Trinity Lutheran Church, Franktown, Colorado

"*We Are Engaged!* gave me an effective scriptural basis for a refreshingly raw dissection of my own heart's longings for love and acceptance in this life that ended with feelings of disappointment and failure. Not only is it an encouraging reminder that Christ is what my heart actually longs for, but in my worst sinful condition I am irresistible to God. He pursues me. This book includes tools for searing self-reflection to help me identify what lies I believe and what idols I put ahead of a relationship with Christ. And more, it reminds me that this love story is about nothing that I have to offer and everything that he does. Now that is great hope!"

—**Darby Ullyatt**, Staff, Lutheran High School, Parker, Colorado

"It was such a joy to hear words of hope, passion, and conviction in God's wonderful larger story. This book guides me to deeper awareness of Trinitarian intimacy to which God invites us. I can envision many believers finding the thoughts, Scripture references, and personal stories lifting them to a richer journey with the Lord."

—**Tom Board**, Marital and Career Counselor

"*We Are Engaged!* is a book that will bring hope to the hopeless, comfort to the comfortless, and peace and pardon to those who have looked for it in all the wrong places. It powerfully demonstrates the comparison of earthly marriage to our eternal marriage with Christ. And it culminates with the glorious truth that the best is yet to come! This book refocused my attention off my sinful flesh and on to the glorious peace and hope that is found in Jesus Christ. Simply put, I loved it!"

—**David Ahlman**, Host, *Daily Truths* Podcast

"*We Are Engaged!* provides food for the soul as it is anchored in God's Word. In his Word we learn just how close Jesus is within us. Craig desires for his readers to experience this close and intimate spiritual union with God through the Lord Jesus Christ. It is a book long overdue. It would be a great adult Bible study. Readers will be on a journey to examine their own lives and walk with God."

—**Larry A. Alb**, MD, Psychiatrist

"*We Are Engaged!* does a beautiful job capturing the essence of our relationship with the triune God. It would be impossible to read this book and not grow in your understanding of the breadth and length and height and depth of the love of Christ that surpasses knowledge. You will also be left with a greater understanding and appreciation of God's plan for your time here on earth and be energized to embrace and live out the purpose God has for your life!"

—**Andrew Hasz**, Head of School, Forge Christian High School, Arvada, Colorado

"Craig writes as he teaches, with passion for the truth, love for our Savior Jesus, and a constant referral to God's Holy Word. *We Are Engaged!* expertly tackles the tough, yet comforting, topics of our sanctification and God's gracious election. This book brings the reader great hope that can be found only in Jesus' cross and resurrection. Are you asking questions like, 'Why did this happen?' 'How could God be at work in this?' 'Is there any hope for me?' If so, this book is for you!"

—**Timothy Oberdieck**, Youth Director, St. John's Lutheran Church and School, Seward, Nebraska

"*We Are Engaged!* leaves the reader hopeful and looking forward to our marriage with Christ, the new earth, and true shalom. The analogies and application from each chapter are helpful and engaging—I am still thinking about Chapter 3 after finishing the book. Craig writes with genuine authenticity which makes it relatable for any person who is poor in spirit (which is all of us) and the questions for reflection allow for deeper connection with our Lord. Such discussions in a small group could be life changing."

—**Alicia Kidston**, Dean of Women, Lutheran High School, Parker, Colorado

We Are Engaged!

We Are Engaged!

Our Love Story With Jesus

Craig Parrott

RESOURCE *Publications* · Eugene, Oregon

Resource Publications
An Imprint of Wipf and Stock Publishers
199 W. 8th Ave., Suite 3
Eugene, OR 97401

www.wipfandstock.com

PAPERBACK ISBN: 979-8-3852-4839-1
HARDCOVER ISBN: 979-8-3852-4840-7
EBOOK ISBN: 979-8-3852-4841-4

VERSION NUMBER 10/24/25

This book is dedicated to the five women God has used the most to woo me increasingly to him:

To my dear mother:

I believe she was eagerly looking forward to her eternal marriage with Jesus and she has inspired me to do the same.

To Linda, Debbie, Rebecca, and Michelle:

I pray that you each have grown in the grace and knowledge of your one, true love, Jesus.

Contents

Acknowledgements | xi

Introduction | 1
Preface—First-Century Engagements | 7
1. God's Proposal and Vow to Us | 15
2. We Need Wedding Clothes and a Makeover | 21
3. We Need to Leave Former Lovers | 28
4. We Need the Gift of Faith | 36
5. We Need the Gift of Hope | 42
6. We Need the Gift of Love | 48
7. We Have a Gift Registry | 54
8. We Have 66 Love Letters | 61
9. We Want to Submit | 67
10. We Need Ongoing Forgiveness | 75
11. We Join His Family | 83
12. We Need a Wedding Planner | 90
13. We Must Talk About Our Beloved | 96
14. We Long, Groan, and Anticipate | 102
15. We Cleave and Become One Flesh | 109

Bibliography | 119

Acknowledgements

I WAS TAUGHT THAT the secret to good writing is rewriting. I was also taught that "With many counselors plans succeed" (Prov 15:22). Thus, there are many names who contributed to this final draft behind the single name that appears on the cover of this book. I would like to thank all of them for what you are reading. I ask in advance for the forgiveness of anyone whose name I will accidentally omit.

I would like to thank the seniors from the Class of 2025 at Lutheran High School in Parker, Colorado, who showed up and did their job as students. Frequently, I hurried home after school and wrote insights that arose from class questions, discussions, and devotions from this faith-filled group of disciples. As Paul told the Romans, I longed to see them every day and exchange mutual encouragement in the faith (Rom 1:11–12).

I would like to thank Joshua Shull, Mark Hollenbeck, Dean Goedeker, Marlene Goedeker, Jon Jorgenson, Dave Fonda, Kim Alb, Rev. Bobby Walston, Alicia Kidston, Daniel Vanderhyde, Andrew Hasz, and Rev. Dave Ahlman. They told me by their reactions that this book could bless people. That affirmation was meaningful because I have seen their faith expressed in love toward God and others.

I would like to thank Marty Kohlwey for the numerous conversations regarding our shared experiences as aging believers and for his affirming the content of this book. He reassured me that I am not alone in my journey.

I am very grateful for the many hours of love and care provided by thoughtful proofreaders such as Darby Ullyatt, Larry Alb, Tim Oberdieck, and Walt Keith. Their sincere, careful, and honest feedback was humbling, and I considered every comment carefully. This is a better book because of their work of faith, labor of love, and steadfastness of hope in our Lord Jesus Christ.

I am very grateful to Caleb Fischer for his proofreading and help footnoting and formatting the manuscript, most of this work done in a twenty-four-hour break between a mission trip and a trip to celebrate a friend's wedding.

I am grateful that God led me to Tom Board, a spiritual mentor for the past twenty-six years. Tom disrupts my fleshly thinking and entices me to walk with the Spirit in me. His endorsement of this book was meaningful and appreciated affirmation.

"A friend loves at all times, but a brother is born for adversity" (Prov 17:17). I am very grateful for the close brothers God has blessed with me with for over twenty-five years: Dave Ahlman, Mark Hollenbeck, and Ken Penny. They have continually, graciously directed my head and heart to Jesus, our Beloved. They have genuinely shared their questions and struggles. They have listened with love and spoken with wisdom from above. They have been Jesus with skin on to me.

I am also grateful for the countless authors, pastors, colleagues, and students over the years who have taught and reminded me of God's truths. I refer to some of them in this book and direct you to their writings in the bibliography. I counsel students to stay close to God's Word and to God's people. Our relationship with our Beloved is fed by such means.

I am grateful for Steve Byrnes from 1517 Publishing, who gave such a hopeful and gracious rejection to my book proposal. It included the recommendation that I approach Wipf and Stock for publication.

I am thankful for the staff at Wipf and Stock for preparing my manuscript for publication and for promoting it to readers who might be blessed by it: Managing Editor Matt Wimer for his patient and quick responsiveness to my queries; Jordan Horowitz for his careful and insightful copyediting; and Calvin Jaffarian for his attentive and gracious typesetting.

Finally, I would like to thank and give all praise and glory to our Beloved, to the lover, redeemer, and renewer of our souls. By his glorious grace and Holy Spirit in me, I loved writing this book. To ponder and contemplate the gospel of God's grace for us in Jesus in each chapter was indeed a delight and a joy. It would give me no greater joy than to know that you, the reader, experience this same joy as you read this book.

Introduction

GETTING ENGAGED TO BE married is one of the most thrilling and exciting times in a person's life. We really can't keep this news quiet. Every fiber of our being wants to shout this news to everyone we know: "We are engaged! My lover loves me and wants to live with me for the rest of our lives! We are going to be married!"

It means we have found someone—or they have found us—who wants to be with us and share life's experiences together, a companion who pledges to love, cherish, and remain with us regardless of what may happen. It means someone will be with us through joys and sorrows, highs and lows, laughter and tears. It means we will have someone to help bear our burdens. It means someone in this world loves us and has chosen to be with us. We can know and be known. We have a best friend. We will not be alone.

But then begins the engagement period. It is not all sunshine and rainbows. It is also a time of pining and longing. It can be filled with impatience and anxiety. It can be plagued with doubts and second guessing. It can be stressful, as the desire for a perfect wedding can be a demanding taskmaster and the details to be attended to can be numerous and overwhelming. There is a lengthy checklist of what needs to be accomplished and a timeline in which to do it.

When all is said and done, the engagement period is a time of preparation and waiting. We are committed to each other, but we cannot yet be with each other completely. We are as good as married, but we are not yet experiencing the face-to-face oneness that is deeply desired. We are getting to know each other better as we prepare to live together. There are light times full of laughter and feeling close, and there are heavy times full of sadness and feeling distant.

And throughout all the time of our engagement, through the personal race marked out for us, desire for the Beloved deepens and intensifies.

This book has been written due to several influences. A good friend, Mark Hollenbeck, suggested that I write something during the last chapter of my time in this world. Then I heard a young colleague give a chapel about his engagement. A few brothers from my men's group at church encouraged me to explore it. Ideas began to percolate. But nothing has influenced me more to contemplate our present state of being engaged to our Lord than my four engagements, four marriages, and four divorces in this world. You see, I am the Samaritan man at the well.

Say whatever you will about that dear woman in John 4—I personally know one thing for sure: her quest for unfailing, steadfast love had repeatedly resulted in a broken heart. She was always left desperately thirsting for more. Jesus knew this, as seen by his invitation to her to drink from him and find living water. It is also one of the rare times in the Gospels when Jesus actually reveals his true identity: "I who speak to you am he (the Messiah)" (John 4:26).

Notice the deep connection happening in this exchange between Jesus and this Samaritan woman. He knows all about her five marriages and present arrangement of cohabiting with a man, and he still desires a relationship with her. He invites her to find in him what she has not been able to find in six men—unfailing, steadfast love. Think about that. On a cosmic level, from the five-hundred-thousand-foot view, Jesus is essentially proposing relationship to this foreign woman.

The Samaritans descended from Israelites who were taken in the Assyrian exile in 722 BC, but the Jews looked down upon them because they intermarried with other captives and forsook some of their Jewish roots. For Jesus to talk to a woman, let alone a Samaritan woman, was culturally taboo. But he risks even more. For him to touch a cup or ladle from her hand to get a drink would make him ceremonially unclean. It would prevent him from worshiping in the temple until he was cleansed. But that does not stop him from moving toward her when he saw her need.

As they talk, he reveals his identity to her, something he kept from Jewish audiences because they expected and wanted an earthly king. He essentially tells her, "I am the Messiah, the one promised for centuries, the chosen one sent to save people from their sins, the one who will reunite God and man forever." Is this not what lovers do? They gradually get more and more vulnerable and honest with each other. They share their secrets.

They thirst to know another and to be known. They thirst to be accepted with grace and love. And the thirst is greater the more unlovable they know themselves to be. They thirst to be accepted by another and to be safe with another. They thirst to matter, to really matter, to someone. Jesus knew the thirst of her heart and he compassionately wanted to quench it.

Our pharisaical judging filter misses the heart of this story when our first thought is that this woman has been sinful. Her being sinful is a given since we all have fallen short of God's glory, whether we have been married six times or for sixty years to one person. How sin has specifically impacted her relationships is not revealed in this dialogue. All we know for certain is they have ended, as all relationships in this broken world eventually do. And the end of a close relationship is sad, tragic, and heartbreaking when it occurs. What we know for certain is that this woman has suffered . . . repeatedly.

Perhaps men in her life died, committed adultery, abandoned her, or abused her. Perhaps they or she ran away when they became unhappy. It just takes one spouse to end a marriage and, in that culture, as in ours today, divorce was too easily achieved. Do the reasons her past relationships ended matter? Our rebellious flesh likes to believe we have more control over making life turn out the way we want it to. Our self-righteous flesh likes to think, "If we just do A, then we will get B," and we can feel proud of the success. Our self-justifying flesh likes to compare ourselves with others, so we feel worthy. Take another careful look at this story. I submit the reasons for what ended her relationships don't matter because they are not given to us. What matters is her life-long thirst for unfailing, steadfast love.

Her several, long-gone relationships have led her to a well in the heat of the day, probably to avoid judgmental looks from people who would draw their water at cooler times, in the morning or evening. And there she finds Jesus, or rather, he finds her. He initiates the conversation with her, as he does with all of us. He knows her heart. He meets her where she is, in all her brokenness and sorrow. He knows all about her pain and thirst and attempts to quench both. Yet, unlike anyone else in her life, he moves toward her, talks very, very personally with her, and invites her into a relationship with him. He fascinates her. He captivates her. She becomes practically giddy, as seen by her leaving her water jar behind (John 4:28). She accepts his offer, and she asks for living water from Jesus so she won't be thirsty ever again (John 4:15).

To the first-century reader, "living water" was moving, fresh, and active. It was a babbling brook, a bubbling spring, or a steadily moving stream. She has finally met a person who will never leave her and a love that will never run out. This man will go to, through, and beyond death. Think about it. What would move her to run to town and talk excitedly to people she had been shamefully avoiding? I believe she felt sparks. She sensed a connection and hope like none other she had ever experienced. She had met the long-anticipated Messiah, the one whose "dominion is an everlasting dominion, which shall not pass away, and his kingdom one that shall not be destroyed" (Dan 7:14). Her heart and soul must have been overflowing with emotions of being accepted, really accepted, and loved—really, truly, deeply loved—for the first time in her life. She had met the fulfillment of her dreams! Jesus knew all that she ever did (John 4:29), and yet he still wanted to be with her! He offered her abundant life with him. She had met her Savior, the Savior of the world (John 4:42). She felt secure and safe in him. And she immediately wanted to tell others about him.

The men she had known in her life up until this time had proven to be "broken cisterns that could not hold water" (Jer 2:13). As demonstrated conclusively by their absence, they did not fulfill this woman's thirst for unfailing, steadfast love. But in Jesus she had finally met the "fountain of living waters" (Jer 2:13).

I believe this story in John 4 is about the compassionate, relentless love of Jesus. Like so many encounters in the Gospel, Jesus saw a need and offered to meet it. The Samaritan woman at the well—and you and I—have prayed, perhaps without realizing it, "O God, you are my God; earnestly I seek you; my soul thirsts for you; my flesh faints for you, as in a dry and weary land where there is no water" (Ps 63:1). This dear woman finally met eternal life, which is the same as knowing God (John 17:3). First Thessalonians 5:10 tells us, "He died for us so that whether we are awake (living) or asleep (dead) we might live with him." Is that not the summary, the essence, the thesis of Genesis to Revelation? What was separated in the garden was reconnected at the cross and is now moving toward renewal, the happily-ever-after our souls desperately long for, when we will live in perfect shalom—peace, harmony, wholeness, unity, oneness—with our lover. We finally have a love that is unfailing and steadfast. In the meantime, where we are now, is the engagement season. Theologians call it the "now-but-not-yet" time.

I am writing this book to fellow travelers who are thirsty. I am writing to those of you who are lonely, who have been rejected, who have failed, or who have lost loves. You are not alone. I am writing to those of you who are pretending that life is better than it is, that your relationships are better than they are. I am encouraging you to let yourself feel the pain and disappointment of your deepest longings, your closest relationships, your greatest dreams. I am writing to those of you who feel a distance from God and who want to be closer. He is closer to you than you realize. I am writing to those of you who are looking for the perfect, fulfilling relationship. I want to tell you, "You have found him! Let me introduce you!" I am writing to those of you who can see God's transforming grace in your lives and to those of you who have been blessed with a pretty good life. Whatever success God has given you out of pure grace has been merely to point you to the greater reality surrounding you. I want to tell you not to rejoice in your good life here but to rejoice that your name is written in heaven (Luke 10:20). Something much, much better lies ahead. And it is way beyond what you could ever ask or imagine.

I have really good news for all of you. There is someone who knows everything you have ever thought, said, or done, and he still wants to be with you. There is someone who knows the deep desires of your heart and he wants to fulfill them. You are engaged to the lover of your soul! The King of kings and Lord of lords has proposed to you, and he wants to live with you forever! He has paid the bride price with his own precious blood. He will never leave you or forsake you. He is preparing a wonderful place for you. Whatever pain or disappointment you are living with right now will not last. Whatever you deeply hunger or thirst for will be satisfied. A wedding celebration for you is coming. "In his presence is the fullness of joy; at his right hand are pleasures forevermore" (Ps 16:11). The best life, the best you, the best relationship, the best family, the best church, the best country, is on the calendar. The Day has been set. And when it arrives, clocks and calendars will be thrown away. There will be no more pain or tears or death. The best is yet to come.

But at present we are bogged down in the land of time. So, what are we to do? We are to do what engaged people do. Prepare and wait. We are to prepare for the big day and the bigger eternity. We are to grow in the grace and knowledge of our Beloved. We are to tell everyone we meet by our words and by our actions how great this guy truly is and the awesome life we have ahead. We are to grow in faith, hope, and love. We are to invite all we can to the wedding. And we are to wait in eager anticipation for our Beloved to finish his preparations and for his return for us. In his last love letter to us, in Revelation 22:20, he wrote, "Surely, I am coming soon."

"The Spirit and the Bride say, 'Come.' And let the one who hears say, 'Come.' And let the one who is thirsty come; let the one who desires take the water of life without price" (Rev 22:17). We are to plead with him in ever-increasing urgency and anticipation, "Come, Lord Jesus!"

For we are engaged! And this is our love story with Jesus.

QUESTIONS FOR DISCUSSION/REFLECTION:

1. What is your reaction to being engaged to Jesus?

2. Ponder the fact that Jesus knows everything about you—every detestable thought, word, and action that you have ever done—and he still wants a relationship with you. What does it mean to you that he is moving toward you rather than away from you?

3. Read John 4:1–42. What have you been thirsting for all your life that only Jesus can fulfill?

4. What relationships have ended in your lifetime? Why did they end? What relationships have not been all you wanted them to be? How have you felt in all the above?

5. Sing or listen to "In Christ Alone."

Preface—**First-Century Engagements**

As YOU CAN SEE, this book is one extended analogy of an earthly engagement prior to a wedding and of our present relationship with Jesus. The idea primarily comes from John 14:2–3, where Jesus told his disciples, "In my Father's house are many rooms . . . I go to prepare a place for you . . . If I go and prepare a place for you, I will come again and will take you to myself, that where I am you may be also." Engaged grooms would return to their father's house and build a room for the couple to live after their wedding. Jesus was essentially telling his disciples that their relationship with him is now like a betrothal and that life together in the new heavens and new earth will be like marriage. The two will be one.

I invite you to explore with me the implications for us believers in this analogy. It is enlightening to go online and research first-century Jewish marriage traditions. After reading several sources, I have found ten fascinating points of comparison. Read this chapter slowly and ponder and marvel at what God has done, is doing, and will do for you, his beloved bride.

1. First of all, the fathers of the bride and groom arranged the marriage. In many ways, it was a business transaction between two families. The father of the son would approach the father of the bride with the proposal of the merger. The father of the son bore the expense of paying the father of the bride a dowry, a bride price. The father of the bride did not pay anything. He merely accepted the offer. The fathers of the two families and the groom would sign a marriage document. Notice that the bride was pretty passive in the entire affair, just as we believers are passive in God's justification for us in Jesus.

In our Western world today, we have moved to the opposite situation: the bride's father pays the greater price, and the day is all about the bride. That actually is a good picture of what sin has done. It has stolen praise, glory, and honor from the Father and the Son and has moved it to us, the bride. Sin makes life all about us. We become selfish, self-centered, and self-absorbed. We want to be our own god. But first-century Jewish custom was closer to the intended spiritual reality. The wedding was all about the actions of the father and the son.

> For God so loved the world, that he gave his only son, that whoever believes in him should not perish but have eternal life. For God did not send his son into the world to condemn the world, but in order that the world might be saved through him. (John 3:16–17)

> You are not your own, for you were bought with a price. (1 Cor 6:19–20)

2. The bride price was not always monetary. It could also be services rendered. You might recall that Jacob worked seven years so he could marry his beloved Rachel. Genesis 29:20 tells us, "So Jacob served seven years for Rachel, and they seemed to him but a few days because of the love he had for her." The seven years became fourteen, as he was tricked by Laban to marry the older, less desirable sister Leah first (Gen 29). I highly recommend reading Tim Keller's *Counterfeit Gods* for a great gospel explanation of that story and its application for us.

As we see from the above example, we can tell how much another loves us by what they are willing to suffer for us. The greatest agony we can experience is losing a relationship that we deeply want. Now ponder the agony Jesus experienced on the cross as he bore our sin and its punishment, separation from the Father. He cried out, "My God, my God, why have you forsaken me?" (Matt 27:46). That is what he was willing to suffer so you and I could be with him for eternity.

Just before Jesus took his last breath on the cross, the temple curtain was torn in two from the top to the bottom. This curtain was sixty feet high, thirty feet wide, and twelve inches thick. Only one person passed through that curtain, and that was only once a year on the Day of Atonement. He was the high priest. Our Beloved's payment for our sin opened the way for us to enter his holy presence.

John 15:13 tells us, "Greater love has no one than this, that a man lay down his life for his friends." You and I have been bought at a very, very great price. It is the very thing that separates Christianity from every other religion. God does the reconciling work. God unites us with him out of sheer grace. He died for us, paying our debt caused by our rebellious sin, in a most brutal fashion on a cross.

> For our sake he made him to be sin who knew no sin, so that in him we might become the righteousness of God. (2 Cor 5:21)

> He himself bore our sins in his body on the tree, that we might die to sin and live to righteousness. By his wounds you have been healed. (1 Pet 2:24)

3. More than the wedding ceremony, the betrothal was the defining moment of identity change for the bride. Although she remained in her father's house, she was legally married to her husband. You might recall that Joseph considered divorcing Mary quietly after learning she was pregnant when they were betrothed (Matt 1:18–19). The marriage contract began simply with a declaration of marriage from the groom to the bride's father.

> But to all who did receive him, who believed in his name, he gave the right to become children of God, who were born, not of blood nor the will of the flesh nor of the will of man, but of God. (John 1:12–13)

> And because of him you are in Christ Jesus, who became to us wisdom from God, righteousness and sanctification and redemption, so that, as it is written, "Let the one who boasts, boast in the Lord." (1 Cor 1:30–31)

4. The couple was never to be alone together or have any physical contact during the engagement period. It is said that 85 to 90 percent of communication is nonverbal. It is the look in one's eye, the tone in the voice, the touch of the hand that conveys so much more than mere words on a page or the text on a phone could ever get across. It brings to mind the story soon after Jesus rose from the dead when he appeared to Mary Magdalene in John 20:17: "Jesus said to her, 'Do not cling to me, for I have not yet ascended to the Father; but go to my brothers and say to them, 'I am ascending to my Father and your Father, to my God and your God.'" The engagement period increases the desire to see, touch, and hold the Beloved. But we must wait for the wedding when he will return for us.

> "For I know that my Redeemer lives, and at the last he will stand upon the earth. And after my skin has been thus destroyed, yet

in my flesh I shall see God, whom I shall see for myself, and my eyes shall behold, and not another. My heart faints within me!" (Job 19:25–27)

The Spirit and the Bride say, "Come." And let the one who hears say, "Come." And let the one who is thirsty come; let the one who desires take the water of life without price. (Rev 22:17)

5. The groom gave gifts to the bride. Love is expressed by giving. Parents enjoy doting on their children, and spouses enjoy lavishing on each other. But if we explore this aspect of first-century engagements, we will see that we have nothing to offer our Beloved. In fact, we bring to this merger nothing but incalculable debt and a death sentence. All the wonderful gifts must come from him to us. And they most certainly do, in abundance.

But earnestly desire the higher gifts . . . So now faith, hope and love abide, these three, but the greatest of these is love. (1 Cor 12:31; 13:13)

Every good gift and every perfect gift is from above, coming down from the Father of lights with whom there is no variation or shadow due to change. (Jas 1:17)

6. The groom would appear by surprise to begin the wedding with a feast. Brides were to be ready for his arrival at any moment. "Then the kingdom of heaven will be like ten virgins who took their lamps and went to meet the bridegroom. Five of them were foolish, and five were wise. For when the foolish took their lamps, they took no oil with them, but the wise took flasks of oil with their lamps. As the bridegroom was delayed, they all became drowsy and slept. But at midnight there was a cry, 'Here is the bridegroom! Come out to meet him.' Then all those virgins rose and trimmed their lamps. And the foolish said to the wise, 'Give us some of your oil, for our lamps are going out.' But the wise answered, saying, 'Since there will not be enough for us and for you, go rather to the dealers and buy for yourselves. And while they were going to buy, the bridegroom came, and those who were ready went in with him to the marriage feast, and the door was shut. Afterward the other virgins came also, saying, 'Lord, lord, open to us.' But he answered, 'Truly, I say to you, I do not know you.' Watch therefore, for you know neither the day nor the hour" (Matt 25:1–13).

This is one reason that I prefer the amillennial view of the end times. In that view, which has been in the church since the third century thanks to Augustine, Jesus could return literally at any moment to take us home to be with him forever. The premillennial view, which has been growing in popularity since the Age of Reason in the seventeenth and eighteenth centuries, believes Jesus has a few more prophecies to fulfill before he will return for us. Some of them are the literal rebuilding of the temple in Jerusalem, a literal thousand-year reign on earth by Jesus, and a time of tribulation. The amillennial view, however, sees Jesus' resurrection as the figurative rebuilding of the temple (John 2:19–22), that he has been reigning with all power and authority from the Father for a figurative one thousand years since his resurrection (Matt 28:18–20), and that the tribulation has been happening for the past two thousand years (Rev 1:9).

> But concerning that day and hour no one knows, not even the angels of heaven, nor the Son, but the Father only. (Matt 24:26)

> For the Lord himself will descend from heaven with a cry of command, with the voice of an archangel, and with the sound of the trumpet of God. And the dead in Christ will rise first. Then we who are alive, who are left, will be caught up together with them in the clouds to meet the Lord in the air, and so we will always be with the Lord. (1 Thess 4:16–17)

7. The bride would have a ritual cleansing prior to the wedding. John 13:8 recounts the story of when Jesus washed the disciples' feet. Peter protested and Jesus said to him, "If I do not wash you, have no share with me." Upon hearing this, Peter then exclaimed, "Lord, not my feet only but also my hands and my head!" (John 13:9). He knew he was a sinful man in great need of cleansing and purifying.

We must be holy, we must be totally pure, in order to stand in the presence of our holy God. Sin separates us from him, and that separation must be removed. A believer can now look upon his or her baptism as the ritual cleansing prior to the wedding. I love witnessing a baptism where the person is completely immersed in a tub for this reason. And upon our death and resurrection, we will receive a new and glorified body, a body that will no longer be subject to sin, death, or deterioration.

> As Christ loved the church and gave himself up for her, that he might sanctify her, having cleansed her by the washing of water with the word, so that he might present the church to himself in splendor, without spot or wrinkle or any such thing, that she might be holy and without blemish. (Eph 5:25–27)

> He saved us, not because of works done by us in righteousness, but according to his own mercy, by the washing of regeneration and renewal of the Holy Spirit. (Titus 3:5)

8. The marital relationship symbolized the covenant between God and Israel that has been fulfilled in the Church. Ephesians 5:31–32 tells us, "Therefore, a man shall leave his father and mother and hold fast to his wife, and the two shall become one flesh. This mystery is profound, and I am saying that it refers to Christ and the church."

Russ Moulds, my mentor who taught me how to teach, liked to say, "Everything on earth is a parable with a heavenly meaning." Everything can be used to teach something about God. Marriage is our most intimate relationship on earth. It is incredible and very revealing of God's heart and plan of salvation that he would use marriage to describe his relationship with us. And as the groom, he chooses us and makes it all happen.

> In speaking of a new covenant, he makes the first one obsolete. And what is becoming obsolete and growing old is ready to vanish away. (Heb 8:8)

> For on the one hand, a former commandment is set aside, because of its weakness and uselessness (for the law made nothing perfect); but on the other hand, a better hope is introduced, through which we draw near to God. (Heb 7:18–19)

9. At their wedding, the engaged couple would drink wine from a common cup to seal the marriage covenant and to signify the joy of their new life together. What do you think about before, during, and after you take the Lord's Supper at your church? The question is much more than an academic one. I think the average believer contemplates all the sins of omission and commission that he or she did recently. The sacrament actually invites us to think about two things: the bride price of forgiveness paid for us by our Beloved's blood and his joyous return for us. What a simple, lovely, precious gift from God to give us a tangible way for our hearts and minds to remember the two most pivotal events in the history of all creation—redemption and restoration.

> The Lord Jesus on the night when he was betrayed took bread, and when he had given thanks, he broke it, and said, "This is my body which is for you. Do this in remembrance of me." In the same way also he took the cup, after supper, saying, "This cup is the new covenant in my blood. Do this, as often as you drink it, in remembrance

of me." For as often as you eat this bread and drink the cup, you proclaim the Lord's death until he comes. (1 Cor 14:23–26)

For this is the blood of the covenant, which is poured out for many for the forgiveness of sins. I tell you I will not drink again of this fruit of the vine until that day when I drink it new with you in my Father's kingdom. (Matt 26:28–29)

10. The wedding essentially changed where the bride lived and allowed her to finally see her husband's face. It is interesting to ponder the "room" in which God is preparing for us to live forever with him. In one sense, it is the new heavens and the new earth. But, in another sense, it is also us. Revelation tells us there is no temple in heaven for God himself will dwell with his people. First Corinthians tells us that we are the temple of the Holy Spirit (1 Cor 6:19). We are presently being transformed, or renovated, to be one with our Beloved. And we will live not only with him but also with his family.

"In my Father's house are many rooms. If it were not so, would I have told you that I go to prepare a place for you? And if I go and prepare a place for you, I will come again and will take you to myself, that where I am you may be also" (John 14:2–3).

"Father, I desire that they also, whom you have given me, may be with me where I am, to see my glory that you have given me because you loved me before the foundation of the world" (John 17:24).

At this point, you might be wondering about some engagement/marriage customs in our present day that I have not mentioned. I have chosen to omit them because many of our current Western practices come from Roman culture and not from our Jewish ancestors' tradition. All the imagery in the Bible refers to Jewish customs and not to Gentile ones.

The analogy I offer in this book, therefore, is not an exhaustive or a complete one. I do not claim to be any kind of expert on Jewish or Roman engagement customs. I simply want to pass along the exciting and thrilling comfort I have found by pondering God's Word and how he speaks of his being engaged to us his chosen. If you derive any enjoyment and encouragement contemplating the same, you know Whom to thank. There is one chapter near the end of the book where I take great liberties and use a rather modern-day convention, and that is of a wedding coordinator or planner. As I wrote the book, it became apparent to me that the Holy Spirit is at work in every step along the way. His energy, influence, and power are in all the details of our engagement, wedding, and marriage. Nothing happens without him.

So, now we are engaged to be married to Jesus. It is the most profound thought we can ever have: "God loves me." Say it to yourself aloud right now. Say it three times, emphasizing each of the three main words: *God* loves me; God *loves* me; God loves *me*! I pray Paul's prayer in Ephesians 3:17–19 for you: "So that Christ may dwell in your hearts through faith—that you, being rooted and grounded in love, may have strength to comprehend with all the saints what is the breadth and length and height and depth, and to know the love of Christ that surpasses knowledge, that you may be filled with all the fullness of God." When this happens, you will discover there is only one time in our life when we should rightfully ask the question, "Why me?" It isn't when we are suffering. It is when we are contemplating the facts that God loves us, has chosen us, and wants to live with us forever.

Let's begin to explore, enjoy, and embrace his love story with us.

QUESTIONS FOR DISCUSSION/REFLECTION:

1. Which of the ten first-century engagement practices got your attention the most? Why?

2. *God* wants to live with *you* in this world and in the world to come. It is why he died for you. How does this truth strike you today?

3. Notice how passive the role of the bride was. What happens when you ponder more what you do for God? What happens when you ponder more what God does for you?

4. When is it most difficult to believe that God loves you? When is it easiest?

5. Sing or listen to "To God Be the Glory."

Chapter 1: **God's Proposal and Vow to Us**

LOVERS MAKE PROMISES. GOOD lovers keep them. Our relationship with God begins and continues solely because of his promise to us. The word in Scripture for "promise" is *covenant*. The word *testament* is another word for *covenant*. Thus, the Bible is divided into two primary covenants, the old and the new. We can see that God likes to make and keep promises.

The first promise we see is the messianic promise to the whole world found in Genesis 3:15: "I will put enmity between you and the woman, and between your offspring and her offspring; he shall bruise your head, and you shall bruise his heel." The second covenant is with Noah and the whole world when God promised to never destroy all living things again by a flood (Gen 8:21–22). God promised Abraham in Genesis 12:1–3: "Go from your country and your kindred and your father's house to the land that I will show you. And I will make you a great nation, and I will bless you and make your name great, so that you will be a blessing. I will bless those who bless you, and him who dishonors you I will curse, and in you all the families of the earth shall be blessed." God promised David that he would have a descendant who would sit on the throne forever (2 Sam 7:16). And God made an old covenant with the nation of Israel, which Israel repeatedly broke (Deut 7:6–11).

Some readers might reasonably wonder, "Why did God make an old covenant, especially if he knew man could not keep the terms?" There are two primary reasons. First, the old covenant made it abundantly clear that no man could keep the law perfectly and thereby save himself. It revealed our inherent unfaithfulness and great need of a Savior. Second, the old covenant pointed people to Christ and the wonderful beauty and relief of the new covenant. God responded with grace to Israel's unfaithfulness by making a new covenant with his people. It was, in essence, a wedding proposal by which God and man could be reunited forever.

> "Behold, the days are coming," declares the Lord, "when I will make a new covenant with the house of Israel and the house of Judah, not like the covenant that I made with their fathers on the day when I took them by the hand to bring them out of the land of Egypt, my covenant that they broke, though I was their husband, declares the Lord. But this is the covenant that I will make with the house of Israel after those days, declares the Lord: I will put my law within them, and I will write it on their hearts. And I will be their God, and they shall be my people . . . For I will forgive their iniquity, and I will remember their sin no more." (Jer 31:31–34)

In the new covenant, God himself makes and keeps the promise. It is unconditional, not conditional as the old one was. This new pact does not depend upon the bride's faithfulness. All she does is believe the groom will do what he promises he will do, and she will receive what he promises. The new covenant removes our sins forever, not temporarily; it allows for Gentiles to be grafted into God's family; it removes us from being under the law and covers us with grace; it energizes people to keep the law by his Spirit within them; and it allows us to directly enter God's presence. The new covenant is instituted by a sinless priest, our Beloved, and was ratified by his own blood and not the blood of animals. It is far superior to the old covenant, for it makes a wedding and marriage between God and us possible. Praise God for the new covenant!

A groom, being head over heels in love with the beloved, strives to have a creative and memorable proposal. He wants it to be special for the one he has chosen to love. He wants to lavish her with love and attention. He takes time and care in planning and plotting how to show his beloved how special she is to him, how much he delights in her. You can hear our Beloved's heart behind his plan of redemption and restoration in the words of Isaiah 54:5–7: "For your Maker is your husband, the Lord of hosts is his name; and the Holy One of Israel is your Redeemer, the God of the whole earth he is called. For the Lord has called you like a wife deserted and grieved in spirit, like a wife of youth when she is cast off, says your God . . . with great compassion I will gather you."

Did you catch the description of us? "Like a wife deserted . . . grieved in spirit . . . like a wife . . . when she is cast off." Our Beloved told us in Matthew 5:3, "Blessed are the poor in spirit, for theirs is the kingdom of heaven." He desires the undesirable! He desires the weak and needy! He has great compassion on us. Zephaniah 3:17 tells us, "The Lord your God is in your midst, a mighty one who will save; he will rejoice over you with gladness; he will quiet you by his love; he will exult over you with loud singing." He loves proposing to people who are unlovable, who have absolutely no boxes checked for why they should be loved and chosen. He loves us simply because he loves us. There is no other reason.

Many Christians can recall the moment when Jesus proposed to them. Many cannot. When did you first meet Jesus? Do you remember? Stop reading and think about it right now. Thank him for coming into your life and choosing to be with *you.*

I was too young to remember, but I relish the story as relayed to me by my mother. Because my father would not step foot in a church, our pastor came to our house one Sunday afternoon and baptized me. Growing up in the Lutheran part of God's family, I was baptized as a baby on October 20, 1957. I have never known a time in my life when I was not engaged. I certainly had times, stages, and seasons, however, when I was much more aware of my engagement. And there were all too many times when I did not think about it much.

Jesus makes it clear in John 15:16: "You did not choose me, but I chose you." Earlier in John 1:12–13, John wrote, "But to all who did receive him, who believed in his name, he gave the right to become children of God, who were born, not of blood nor of the will of the flesh nor of the will of man, but of God." The above anecdote drives home the point for me. Jesus literally came to my house to propose to me. And, like first-century engagements, the wedding was arranged by the father without a word from the bride. I was barely a month old at the time.

In the present day, the custom is for the groom to give the bride a ring, signifying that she is spoken for or taken. But our engagement to Jesus is on a cosmic level. Our only other suitor is satan. Therefore, "it is God who establishes us with you in Christ, and has anointed us and who has also put his seal on us and given us his Spirit in our hearts as a guarantee" (2 Cor 1:21–22). What is his seal? His Spirit. What is guaranteed? His faithfulness. His protection and provision for us assures us that we will get to the wedding and to the marriage beyond. John 10:28 gives us one of the sweetest promises from our Beloved in all his 66 Love Letters to us: "I give them eternal life, and they will never perish. No one can snatch them out of my hand." This is the security that we all crave.

When life in this world presents you with feelings of loneliness, unworthiness, or doubt, look to the sure and certain promises of our Beloved:

He is indeed with us always, even till the end of the age.	Matt 28:20
He will never leave us or forsake us.	Heb 13:5
He is working for our good in all things.	Rom 8:28–29
He is faithful and just and will forgive us and cleanse us from all unrighteousness.	1 John 1:9
He who began a good work in you, will bring it to completion at the day of Jesus Christ.	Phil 1:6
He will one day wipe away every tear and remove death, mourning, crying, and pain.	Rev 21:4
He is coming back soon.	Rev 22:7

Ours is the love story of all love stories. Our Beloved is the personification of love. Our Beloved has been planning to marry us for a *very long* time. In fact, before creation, according to Ephesians 1:4–14:

> Even as he chose us in him before the foundation of the world, that we should be holy and blameless before him. In love he predestined us for adoption as sons through Jesus Christ, according to the purpose of his will, to the praise of his glorious grace, with which he has blessed us in the Beloved. In him we have redemption, through his blood, the forgiveness of our trespasses, according to the riches of his grace, which he lavished upon us, in all wisdom and insight making known to us the mystery of his will, according to his purpose, which he set forth in Christ as a plan for the fullness of time, to unite all things in him, things in heaven and on earth.
>
> In him we have obtained an inheritance, having been predestined according to the purpose of him who works all things according to the counsel of his will, so that we who were the first to hope in Christ might be to the praise of his glory. In him you also, when you heard the word of truth, the gospel of your salvation, and believed in him, were sealed with the promised Holy Spirit, who is the guarantee of our inheritance until we acquire possession of it, to the praise of his glory.

Jesus is the lover of all lovers. Can you imagine his creativity, patience, longsuffering, and love? He chose to win our heart by showing the depth of his. He chose literally to go to hell and back for us. "What wondrous love is this, o my soul?" "Amazing grace, how sweet the sound, that saved a wretch like me!" What other love songs come to your mind? They all point our soul to him. He is, after all, our only true, eternal soulmate.

Acts 17:24–28 tells us that God determined the exact time and place where we would live in hopes that we might reach out and find him. Wow. And this passage is clear that God does not need us; more importantly, he wants us. Who would want it any other way? It is the sign of a good, healthy partner. He is self-controlled; that is, he is not controlled by anything outside himself. He is true to himself and his character. And this passage shows us our purpose for being created: it is to be with him.

"The God who made the world and everything in it, being Lord of heaven and earth, does not live in temples made by man, nor is he served by human hands, as though he needed anything, since he himself gives to all mankind life and breath and everything. And he made from one man every nation of mankind to live on the face of the earth, having determined allotted periods and the boundaries of their dwelling place, that they should seek God, in the hope that they might feel their way toward him and find him. Yet, he is actually not far from each one of us, for in him we live and move and have our being" (Acts 17:24–28). Greater words between lovers have never been exchanged in the history of the world. He is indeed our all in all. We have no life apart from him. He is our very life. And he *wants* to live with us!

His proposal and vow to us changes our identity. We have a new name. The God of this universe has chosen and redeemed us to live with him for eternity. We are his chosen ones. We are no longer defined by our successes or failures. We are no longer defined by what we have or don't have. We are no longer defined by any ephemeral role we play in this world. We are no longer defined by our sin. Thanks to the grace, mercy, and love of our Beloved, we now have an identity that endures and surpasses all things and gives us inestimable worth and value. We are the bride-to-be of Christ.

If only one book would serve as our engagement announcement, it could very well be the last one of the 66 Love Letters, Revelation. In Revelation 12:4b–6 and 10–12a we read, "She gave birth to a male child, one who is to rule all the nations with a rod of iron, but her child was caught up to God and to his throne, and the woman fled into the wilderness, where she has a place prepared by God, in which she is to be nourished for 1,260 days . . . And I heard a loud voice in heaven, saying, 'Now the salvation and the power and the kingdom of our God and the authority of his Christ have come, for the accuser of our brothers has been thrown down, who accuses them day and night before our God. And they have conquered him by the blood of the Lamb and by the word of their testimony, for they loved not their lives even unto death. Therefore, rejoice, O heavens and you who dwell in them!'"

God has prepared our engagement time for us. He is nourishing us with all that we need before the wedding. He has come for us not to accuse or condemn us but to save us (John 3:17).

But as we look in the mirror, we can't help but notice that we have a huge problem. And it must be solved, or there will not be a wedding for us.

QUESTIONS FOR DISCUSSION/REFLECTION:

1. Matthew 23:37 reads, "O Jerusalem, Jerusalem, the city that kills the prophets and stones those who are sent to it! How often would I have gathered your children together as a hen gathers her brood under her wings, and you would not!" How long did you refuse God's proposal for relationship in your life?

   How reluctant have you been to fully, whole-heartedly respond with "yes!" to him? What in this world clutches at you for your first-place devotion?

2. At what point in your life did your relationship with Jesus become more alive? What were the circumstances?

3. Which promises from God have been especially meaningful to you in your life? Which ones are carrying you today? Read Matthew 5:6 for another sweet one.

4. Think about it: God was thinking about *you* before he made creation. He chose when and where you would live in hopes you would find him. "You are not your own. You were bought with a price" (1 Cor 6:19). What could possibly give your life more meaning or purpose than this? What is your reaction to his love for you today? Tell him.

5. Sing or listen to "Amazing Grace."

Chapter 2: **We Need Wedding Clothes and a Makeover**

THE FIRST THING WE realize when we get engaged to Jesus is that we have absolutely nothing to wear to the wedding and we need a makeover of epic proportions. The average bride-to-be wants to get a manicure, lose a few pounds, and style her hair. But our needed change goes far beyond cosmetic alterations to our chassis. We need a complete and total overhaul of our engine. As the engagement period lengthens and time goes on, we become more and more aware of our unsightly blemishes and ugly parts. Just when one seems to disappear, another one comes into view. Indeed, the increasing awareness of how unlovable we truly are only serves to heighten the gracious love of our Beloved that moves him regardless to want to be with us. We are unlovable, but we are not unloved. It is much more comforting and restful for our hearts to focus on his love for us rather than on our unloveliness or on our weak love for him.

Our condition could not be worse. Romans 8:5–8 describes us like this: "For those who live according to the flesh set their minds on the things of the flesh, but those who live according to the Spirit set their minds on the things of the Spirit. For to set the mind on the flesh is death, but to set the mind on the Spirit is life and peace. For the mind that is set on the flesh is hostile to God, for it does not submit to God's law; indeed, it cannot. Those who are in the flesh cannot please God." We are dead, hostile, and unable to do anything to please him.

Isaiah 64:6 describes our dire situation like this: "We have all become like one who is unclean, and all our righteous deeds are like a polluted garment." Most commentators say that "polluted garment" in the

Hebrew is describing the cloth used for a woman's menstrual period. It is not simply a matter that our thoughts, words, or actions are wrong. *We are wrong.* Our heart is wrong. Jesus said it like this in Mark 7:20–23: "What comes out of a person is what defiles him. For from within, out of the heart of man, come evil thoughts, sexual immorality, theft, murder, adultery, coveting, wickedness, deceit, sensuality, envy, slander, pride, foolishness. All these evil things come from within, and they defile a person." In other words, sin has made us very, very ugly, depraved, and corrupt. We have no purity in ourselves by which to even think we have the right to wear white on our wedding day.

Paul described our and his situation like this in Philippians 3:8–9: "I count everything as loss because of the surpassing worth of knowing Christ Jesus my Lord. For his sake I have suffered the loss of all things and count them as rubbish, in order that I may gain Christ and be found in him, not having a righteousness of my own that comes from the law, but that which comes through faith in Christ." In other words, we have absolutely no goodness of our own on which to stand either today or on the day of our wedding. Anything that we or the world might perceive as good is "rubbish." The Greek word is "dung." Not only are we ugly but we also stink.

In Ephesians 2:1–3 Paul described us like this: "And you were dead in the trespasses and sins in which you once walked, following the course of this world, following the prince of the power of the air, the spirit that is now at work in the sons of disobedience—among whom we all once lived in the passions of our flesh, carrying out the desires of the body and the mind, and were by nature children of wrath, like the rest of mankind."

The next two words might be the most important words in the entire Bible. "But God." Darrell Johnson, in his book *Ephesians*, says, "This little phrase is the Gospel in the simplest form."[1] These two words describe and capture the life, the real life, of every believer. "But God." Ephesians 2:4–6 continues, "*But God*, being rich in mercy, because of the great love with which he loved us, even when we were dead in our trespasses, made us alive together with Christ—by grace you have been saved." We need to be born again and, thanks be to God, we have been. And it was nothing but pure grace—undeserved favor—on God's part.

Reread Ephesians 2:1–10 right now. If you want to stop reading this book, you have just seen the essence of its message. This is the most concise explanation of our being engaged to our Beloved that we can find. We

1. Johnson, *Ephesians*, 107.

simply do not realize, without God's help and revelation from the Spirit, how bad our sin truly is and how dire our situation truly is. And that means it is also therefore impossible for us to grasp, without the help and revelation of the Spirit, how truly great and awesome our Beloved's love for us is. He has resurrected us from the dead and raised us to life with him. We are his work of art created in Christ to do good works which he has prepared.

Foremost among those good works is faith in him (John 6:29). Every older believer I have ever known reports that they see more of their sin than ever before. They see with greater clarity how they sinned in the past, especially in instances when they believed at the time that they were totally innocent. And they have come to know their flesh as utterly helpless and impotent. Such bankruptcy pushes them to look to our Beloved all the more for grace and mercy. With David they cling to our only Hope: "A broken and contrite heart, O God, you will not despise" (Ps 51:17).

Therefore, it is really evidence of our fleshly arrogance and ignorance that we even dare speak about having any "free will." Luther, of course, said there was no such thing in his *The Bondage of the Will*. Our sinful nature cannot do anything but sin. Our Beloved's heart toward such weak and needy people is seen in Matthew 11:28: "Come to me, all who labor and are heavy laden, and I will give you rest. Take my yoke upon you, and learn from me, for I am gentle and lowly in heart, and you will find rest for your souls." Dane Ortlund has observed in his book *Gentle and Lowly*, "What did he do when he saw the unclean? What was his first impulse when he came across prostitutes and lepers? He moved toward them. Pity flooded his heart, the longing of true compassion."[2]

We must know that we are not righteous but are trapped in the worst of sins—unbelief. Jesus alone is righteous. Sin is unbelief and the refusal to trust in God. We are hardwired in Adam's image to seek our life in anything and everything except God. All of us are fractured in every way, in every aspect of our being. "But God." Jesus touched unclean people and made them clean. He loves the unwanted, the unsightly, the unlovable. He chose us out of his great mercy. He is our husband, and we are his bride. He is enamored with us—even and especially those of us who have failed, been rejected, or been ignored. He is gentle and moves toward the lowly.

Our Beloved does for us what we cannot do for ourselves. It is found in his wedding vow to us in Ezekiel 36:25–27: "I will sprinkle clean water on you, and you shall be clean from all your uncleannesses, and from all

---

2. Ortlund, *Gentle and Lowly*, 31.

your idols I will cleanse you. And I will give you a new heart, and a new spirit I will put within you. And I will remove the heart of stone from your flesh and give you a heart of flesh. And I will put my Spirit within you and cause you to walk in my statutes and be careful to obey my rules." Did you notice what our Beloved has given us? We now have cleansing, a new heart, new spirit, and God's Spirit in us. We are a new creation.

Note the description of our wedding attire in Revelation 19:6–8: "Then I heard what seemed to be the voice of a great multitude, like the roar of many waters and like the sound of mighty peals of thunder, crying out, 'Hallelujah! For the Lord our God the Almighty reigns. Let us rejoice and exult and give him the glory, for the marriage of the Lamb has come, and his Bride has made herself ready; it was granted her to clothe herself with fine linen, bright and pure—' for the fine linen is the righteous deeds of the saints."

I mourn that my body is wasting away, *but God* is renewing me inwardly, day by day.

I mourn that I continue to commit sins I don't want to commit, *but God* has defeated those sins with the perfect righteousness of Christ, who said "no" to them when he was tempted. I mourn that I have no goodness in me, *but God* does righteous deeds through me. I mourn that some family and friends have left me, *but God* will never leave me or forsake me. I mourn over the fallenness of this world, *but God* is making new heavens and a new earth.

The makeover is a flowery way of saying sanctification, the progressive purifying of us in thought, word, and action throughout our entire lives and keeping us in the one true faith. Paul reveals a most amazing truth about what happens to us over the course of the engagement period: "And we all, with unveiled face, beholding the glory of the Lord, are being transformed into the same image from one degree of glory to another. For this comes from the Lord who is the Spirit" (2 Cor 3:18). And he gives the Thessalonians and us this sweet assurance: "May the God of peace himself sanctify you completely and may your whole spirit and soul and body be kept blameless at the coming of our Lord Jesus. He who calls you is faithful; he will surely do it" (1 Thess 5:23–24).

Paul continues the ongoing makeover talk in 2 Corinthians 4:16: "So we do not lose heart. Though our outer self is wasting away, our inner self is being renewed day by day." In Colossians 1:21–23, he states how drastic the change is: "And you, who once were alienated and hostile in mind, doing evil deeds, he has now reconciled in his body of flesh by his death, in order to present you holy and blameless and above reproach before him, if indeed you continue in the faith, stable and steadfast, not shifting from the hope of the gospel that you heard." We must be perfectly holy to stand in the presence of our holy God. This Colossians passage gives us the clothing we need for the wedding. It is our Beloved Jesus himself. Look to him and how he is clothed with perfect righteousness. He offers that spotless, beautiful garment to us in faith.

And that is good because he is perfectly holy and pure to the core of his being. You might recall that no one in the Old Testament could see God's face and live because of their sinfulness. He had mercy on Moses and allowed him to see his back. "I will make all my goodness pass before you and will proclaim before you my name 'The Lord' . . . But . . . you cannot see my face, for man shall not see me and live" (Exod 34:19–20). In addition, 1 Peter 1:16 tells us, "You shall be holy, for I am holy." We need a makeover of epic proportions, and thanks be to God, he gives it to us in Christ.

The entire engagement period is when God is making us positionally holy and progressively more holy. It is rather important, for Hebrews 12:14 tells us, "Strive for . . . holiness without which no one will see the Lord." *Holy* means "separate" or "set apart." From what are we separate or set apart? Believers in Christ are no longer of the world. Nor are we followers of satan. Nor do we live for ourselves. For what are we set apart? We are now called and empowered to live righteously as our Beloved does.

It is worth noting, however, how Matthew 25:37–40 describes our transformation: "Then the righteous will answer him, saying, 'Lord, when did we see you hungry and feed you, or thirsty and give you drink? And when did we see you a stranger and welcome you, or naked and clothe you? And when did we see you sick or in prison and visit you?' And the King will answer them, 'Truly, I say to you, as you did it to one of the least of these my brothers, you did it to me.'" This means that much of our change will be hidden from us. Much of our change will be gradual and slow. And much of our change will be internal. Rather than taking our spiritual pulse often or measuring our growth, it is better to trust our Beloved's word that he is living in us (Gal 2:20) and that he is being formed in us (Gal 4:19). The fruit of change is of the Spirit, not of our labors (Gal 5:22).

So, try this the next time you find yourself fixating on your body of death that clings to you and your ugly sinfulness and sins. Look at the beautiful, perfect righteousness of Jesus. Look at his good deeds. Look at his defeat of evil. Look at his perfection and holiness. Look at his perfect obedience unto death. Look at his glorious resurrection. Look at his faithful promises. And remember your baptism, "For as many of you as were baptized into Christ have put on Christ" (Gal 3:27). Praise be to God! What is his is now ours.

A current expression is so appropriate here: we married up, *very* up. Our Beloved is so out of our league. Theologians have called it "the great exchange." Our Beloved took our putrid, tattered rags of sin and gave us his spotless, clean righteousness. He took our sentence of death and gave us abundant life. In fact, the greater the disparity between us, the greater the praise, glory, and honor that will be due his name at the wedding and for eternity. Our love story with Jesus is the ultimate rags-to-riches story.

Isaiah 61:10 is a perfect final word on this chapter: "I will greatly rejoice in the Lord; my soul shall exult in my God, for he has clothed me with the garments of salvation; he has covered me with the robe of righteousness, as a bridegroom decks himself like a priest with a beautiful headdress, and as a bride adorns herself with her jewels."

Sin has separated us from our Beloved and made us ugly, unloving, and reprehensible. *But God* has reconciled us and given us the perfect, spotless dress and makeover for our wedding. It is the beautiful, loving, and captivating adornment of himself.

QUESTIONS FOR DISCUSSION/REFLECTION:

1. What aspect of your fleshy behavior/thinking is especially repulsive to you today? Read Matthew 5:3 and 5:6. What promises does God give to those who believe they need a makeover?

2. Read Ephesians 2:1–10. You have been "made alive with Christ," "been raised up and seated with him in the heavenly places in Jesus," "been saved," and "created for good works which God prepared beforehand." Notice it is all God's doing. Pause and thank him now for these gifts of his grace.

3. What parts of your life today are you tempted to lean on for your own righteousness? Repent to him now for such pride. Paul counted his good works as "rubbish," and he clung to the righteousness of Jesus that was his by faith in the Lord. Think about his goodness that is now credited to you by faith. Thank him.

4. For the next week, wake up each day and envision putting on the armor of God (Eph 6:14–17). Your helmet is the salvation of Jesus, your breastplate is the righteousness of Jesus, your belt is the truth of Jesus, and your shoes are the gospel of peace in Jesus. He has you covered from head to toe.

5. Sing or listen to "My Hope is Built on Nothing Less."

Chapter 3: **We Need to Leave Former Lovers**

ONE OF THE MOST quoted biblical passages of all, largely because it is used in Christian weddings, is Genesis 2:24: "Therefore a man shall leave his father and his mother and hold fast to his wife, and they shall become one flesh." Some see marriage as a three-step process of leaving, cleaving, and weaving. We obviously cannot hold fast to someone if we are still clinging to someone else. It is the necessary step of leaving former attachments that I want us to explore and contemplate in this chapter.

Whatever we set our heart on and trust in is truly our god. Engagement is the time for us to sever our primary affection with former lovers. It is time to demote them to their rightful place in the hierarchy of our heart. They all fall so far short of the real love we now enjoy with our Beloved. The problem is twofold: we have so many of them and all of them are demanding stalkers. All of them have a very firm grip on first place in our heart. Our predecessors faced the same problem as seen in Jeremiah 2:13: "My people have committed two evils: they have forsaken me, the fountain of living waters, and hewed out cisterns for themselves, broken cisterns that can hold no water."

Are there any harder words to hear for born idolaters than these in Matthew 10:37? "Whoever loves father or mother more than me is not worthy of me, and whoever loves son or daughter more than me is not worthy of me." The point is that none of us *are* worthy of God's love; none of us deserve to be engaged to him. We love so many things, especially good things, more than we love God. Yet, by his great grace, mercy, and compassion, he loves us. He loves us because of who he is, not because of who we are. That is why we can be so confident in our relationship with him. He has unfailing, steadfast love for us. Nothing can separate us from his love for us (Rom 8:39).

Our Beloved, as our ultimate protector and provider, helps us identify our idols. He leads us to see the answers to some questions that drive some of our most oppressive thoughts:

What do we most fear losing?

What, if we lost it, would make us feel that life is no longer worth living?

What subject can make us uncontrollably angry, anxious, or despondent?

What subject paralyzes us from having any objective discussion or criticism around it?

What do we habitually think about to get joy and comfort?

What do our minds drift to when we lie awake in bed?

What do we spend much of our time, energy, and finances on?

What would tempt us to be immoral or unloving in order to procure or keep it?

What do other people have that we tend to covet?

What do we find ourselves praying for that is nowhere promised to us in the Bible?

Idols are cruel taskmasters. They move us to lie, cheat, and steal. They move us to have sex outside marriage. They move us to rage with anger and be unforgiving. They move us to be ungrateful. They move us to leave churches, spouses, and jobs. They destroy marriages, families, friendships, health, finances, and ministries. They move us away from our Beloved. Idols might very well be the number one weapon our enemy uses to steal, kill, and destroy.

God wants the very best for us and that is himself. The engagement time prepares us for eternity with him in his Father's house, and much of that preparation is his prying our grip off things in this world. Recall the promise and vow he has made to us in Ezekiel 36:25, 28: "I will sprinkle clean water on you, and you shall be clean from all your uncleannesses, and from all your idols I will cleanse you . . . You shall be my people, and I will be your God." A big part of our engagement period is for our Beloved to cleanse us from *all* our idols. He and he alone is to have first place in our heart.

Many brides feel pressure as soon as they are engaged. The to-do list immediately forms in the mind. But notice who does all this action in the New Covenant. "I will . . . I will . . . I will." The preparation in this engagement period is done by our Beloved. He prepares us. Notice the passive verb in Revelation 21:2–3: "And I saw the holy city, new Jerusalem, coming down out of heaven from God, *prepared* as a bride adorned for her husband. And I heard a loud voice from the throne saying, 'Behold, the dwelling place of God is with man. He will dwell with them, and they will be his people, and God himself will be with them as their God." Eden, paradise, will be restored. God will walk with us in restored shalom—perfect peace, harmony, wholeness, unity, and oneness.

So, an important step that needs to be repeated throughout our entire time in this world is to leave fearing, loving, or trusting anything or anyone more than we fear, love, and trust our Beloved. Our life is a constant turning from lesser lovers to turn toward and gaze upon the beauty of our greater lover. God is weaning us from loving this world more than we love him. It is both painful and healing, humbling and exalting, dying and enlivening. In fact, Revelation tells us that we are now in the time of tribulation (Rev 1:9). That word means "crushing pressure" as two forces collide. Those forces are the lesser lovers in this world vying with our one, true love for top place in our hearts. We are being liberated from captivity. It is the ultimate exodus before entering the eternal promised land.

Despite our foolish, fleshly efforts to the contrary, we cannot serve two masters (Matt 6:24). Loving our Beloved first and foremost demands that we yield our desires and identities to God's providence and sovereignty. There's hardly a scarier or more difficult thing to do. It feels as if we are dying, and in a real, spiritual sense, we are. The Old Adam and our idols are being crucified. The most painful times in our lives are times in which our idols are being threatened or removed. As Tim Keller has written, "Sometimes God seems to be killing us when he's actually saving us. We don't realize Jesus is all we need until Jesus is all we have."[1]

All of us live for something; all of us love something; all of us trust something for our well-being. It is how we were created, with a vacuum-shaped hole in our soul that must be filled. The original design was for God to fill it. Since the fall in the garden, it has been filled by anything and everything

1. Keller, *Counterfeit Gods*, 19–20.

except him. It is our enemy's favorite deception to take something good for us and make it god to us. His favorite lie is that we need something or someone more than we need our Beloved, that something or someone else will fulfill us more than he will. We need the Holy Spirit to direct our hearts and minds repeatedly to our Beloved, so we love him more than we love our idols. *Love* is listed first in the cluster of fruit given to us by the Spirit.

I suspect that you might have wondered in the introduction what was wrong with me to have had four divorces. Many people typically wonder, "Was it adultery? Did he have a drinking problem? Did he have anger issues?" Our minds can parade the usual suspects and judge. However, the gift of time and some illumination from the Lord has allowed me to see now that idolatry is behind most conflict between people. I can see it more clearly in the rearview mirror. I believe most of what blocks love in our fallen world, both toward God and toward others, is loving some good gift from God too much. We believe satan's lie that we need something for our wellbeing, and then we do whatever it takes to get it, no matter the cost, including abandoning a spouse. The spiritual forces of evil tempt us to demonize and hate whoever we perceive is preventing us from having an idol we believe we must have (Eph 6:12).

In my first marriage, I now see that I loved my workplace and my career more than I loved my wife and children. I looked for my identity, satisfaction, security, and significance there instead of in our Beloved. I became angry and bitter when my second workplace was not living up to my expectations, to my demands. I turned inward and selfish in a pity party and withdrew from loving my wife and children, who should have had clear and unquestioned priority over my work. I married too quickly in a rebound relationship in my second marriage because I feared living alone without sex the rest of my life. I trust you see the idols in my heart there. In retrospect, I believe the idols of family, children, and happiness led to the dissolution of my last two marriages. In summary, marriages end when a spouse loves something more than they love their spouse, and the situation becomes intolerable and hopeless for one of the two.

In all the above scenarios, my ex-wives and I were paralyzed from being able to have the necessary conversations to resolve the tensions due to the grip of idolatry on our hearts. The idol created an emotional minefield full of blind spots. Any discussion was avoided or approached as win/lose rather than win/win. Objectivity was impossible, and all-or-nothing thinking prevailed because we believed we needed the object of our greatest affection. It had become our identity and could not be challenged or criticized. The painful rejection and failure I experienced in divorce, however, was used by God to show me how terrible my idolatry is in my relationship with him. It is simply wrong and evil to love anything or anyone, no matter how good it or they are, more than I love my Creator, Redeemer, and Sanctifier. And he is the only one who can give me the stable identity that I need, one that is not threatened by success or failure or by others' approval or disapproval.

Augustine, and later Luther, maintained that the overarching sin is the first commandment: "You shall have no other gods before me" (Deut 5:7). Breaking any commandment after the first one is also a violation of the first one as well. Augustine said that disordered loves was the cause of much pain and trouble in the world. In my parents' marriage, for example, I can see how my father loved making money more than he loved my mother, sister, brother, and me. I have observed how disordered loves in the lives of friends, coworkers, parents, and students caused much pain and conflict. It hurts to discover that someone close to us loves something or someone more than they love us. It prevents them from loving us better. It is the epitome of betrayal. Imagine what our idolatry does to the heart of God. He created us, he gives us all our good gifts, and he died a most gruesome death so that we might be saved from eternal damnation. He alone is most worthy of our praise, worship, and undivided devotion.

The amazing part in this process is this: the broken heart that results from our loving an idol is a crucial step and great motivator to move us to love more the one, true love who will never leave us or forsake us. We need to discover, usually very painfully so, that whatever we have been relying upon for our life, meaning, peace, joy, and happiness simply does not and cannot fulfill us to the degree that we crave and need. At that point, we have four choices:

1. blame and hate others for blocking what we believed we needed;

2. blame and hate ourselves for failing to procure what we believed we needed;

3. blame and hate God for not cooperating with our plans to get what we believed we needed; or

4. seek the Lord with all our heart to be the life and identity we need and trust that he is working for our good, even when we or others fail.

The letter to Ephesus in Revelation 2:4 speaks to all of us: we have abandoned our first love. In his first epistle, John tells us believers, "In this is love, not that we have loved God but that he loved us and sent his Son to be the propitiation for our sins . . . By this we know that we abide in him and he in us, because he has given us of his Spirit . . . So we have come to know and to believe the love that God has for us . . . By this is love perfected with us, so that we may have confidence for the day of judgment" (1 John 4:10, 13, 16, 17). What we deeply desire—unfailing, steadfast love—can be found only in God. No one can or ever will love us more.

What can we do to fix our dilemma, to love God with all our heart, soul, mind, and strength? By this point in your life, it is probably obvious that we cannot stir up more love for God by any force of our will. We are too broken and self-absorbed. We know Paul's words all too well in Romans 7; 19, 24–25: "For I do not do the good I want, but the evil I do not want is what I keep on doing . . . Wretched man that I am! Who will deliver me from this body of death? Thanks be to God through Jesus Christ our Lord!" Jesus has loved God the Father with all his heart, soul, mind, and strength for us, in our place. He loved him to the point of dying for him, obeying his will to the cross.

Furthermore, Exodus 20:5 describes our Beloved as "jealous." In this world, that word has negative overtones but, if we think about it, our Beloved is the only one in the universe who has a right to be jealous. The dictionary sitting on my desk defines *jealous* as being "vigilant in guarding a possession."[2] The Hebrew word connotes zealous protection over what is rightfully one's own. His jealousy is out of his love and grace for us. We belong to him. He made us and bought us with his precious blood. He wants the best for us. And he is the best for us.

My parents have come and gone. Four wives have come and gone. Children have come and gone. Friends have come and gone. Workplaces have come and gone. Youthfulness has come and gone. Wealth has come and gone. Health has come and gone. Only he has remained. And his grace is what allows us to say with the psalmist, "Whom have I in heaven but you? And there is nothing on earth that I desire besides you. My flesh and my heart may fail, but God is the strength of my heart and my portion forever" (Ps 73:25–26).

Colossians 1:17 tells us that Jesus "is before all things, and in him all things hold together." Other worldviews do not sufficiently explain

2. *Merriam-Webster English Dictionary* (1996), s.v. "jealous."

the cause of pain and suffering we undergo in this world. Health issues, relational breakdowns, and our selfish failures aren't caused by our not being communists or espousing Islam. They are not caused from karma. And they are not meaningless, random, or natural as secularistic evolution maintains. We know tears, mourning, and death are the result of our trying to get life apart from God.

Colossians 1:18 tells us our Beloved "is the head of the body, the church. He is the beginning, the firstborn from the dead, that in everything he might be preeminent." He is now our solution and is working toward making a new world with new creatures to inhabit with him. That is what we really want as seen by our fleshly desire to make parents, spouses, children, and friends in this world be perfect and be God for us. They can't be, however, because they are not him; they only point us to him.

Jesus tells us in Matthew 16:25, "Whoever loses his life for my sake will find it." The engagement period is important and vital, as it helps us experience this transformation of our heart. We must leave former loves in second place before we can cleave and be one flesh with our Beloved. Despite the temptation to return to Egypt, we must leave this world behind. It must be repeated: to love anything or anyone more than we love the God who created us and died for us is evil and wicked at the lowest depth. It is shameful adultery. Yet, that is the essence of sin that clings to us. Hence, our leaving lesser lovers in this world will be a lifelong process. It will become complete only when we totally leave this world and this earth suit of sin.

Judas loved money more than he loved our Savior. Until the Holy Spirit came into him, Peter loved his own life more than he loved our Savior. I have loved marriage, career, sex, comfort, money, food, health, reputation, and countless other things more than I have loved our Beloved. What are you loving today more than you love Jesus? How is it hurting your relationships with others and your giving them a taste of the love of God through you? How is it hurting you? The words of "Come Thou Fount of Every Blessing" come to mind as we close this chapter:

> Oh, to grace how great a debtor, daily I'm constrained to be.
> Let Thy goodness like a fetter, bind my wandering heart to Thee.
> Prone to wander, Lord, I feel it. Prone to leave the God I love.
> Here's my heart, Lord, take and seal it. Seal it for Thy courts above.[3]

---

3. Amazing Hymns, "Come Thou Fount of Every Blessing."

Paul prayed for the Thessalonians, "May the Lord direct your hearts to the love of God and to the steadfastness of Christ" (2 Thess 3:5). The engagement period is the time for us to have our top allegiance shifted to him in grateful response for his allegiance to us. It is time to repent and return to our first love. We must love him more. And that requires a gift that we need from him.

QUESTIONS FOR DISCUSSION/REFLECTION:

1. What do you believe are your top idols at this point in time? Ask yourself the questions listed in this chapter.

2. Count the cost of your idols. How have they caused conflict, problems, or hurt others in your life? Ponder how much time, money, and anxiety you have spent on them.

3. Read Luke 10:38–42. What do you think Martha might have believed she needed for her life and wellbeing? With whom did she become angry and demanding? Have you ever been angry at God? To what idol were you clinging at the time?

   Read John 12:1–6 for a later story in Martha's life. What has remained the same? What has changed? What person in this story wrongly believes he needs something? What is his idol? Notice his attitude toward Jesus.

4. Are you relying on your fleshly performance, rather than Christ's, to give you satisfaction, security, and significance? Read Romans 7:1—8:11 to see the joyous news that you now are married to Another and not to the law.

5. Sing or listen to "Come Thou Fount of Every Blessing."

Chapter 4: **We Need the Gift of Faith**

As I NEAR THE eighth decade of living in this world, it seems to me the Spirit has been doing two primary works in my life. First, he has been convicting me, through an ever-deepening awareness of my fleshly penchant toward idolatry, that I desperately need a Savior. Second, he has been assuring me, through an ever-deepening awareness of God in his Word and his people, that I have one. The former awareness is most humbling; the latter is most comforting. Paul described it in Romans 5:20–21 this way: "Now the law came in to increase the trespass, but where sin increased, grace abounded all the more, so that, as sin reigned in death, grace also might reign through righteousness leading to eternal life through Jesus Christ our Lord."

I can now see why Luther believed God does only two primary works, he kills, and he resurrects. Matthew 23:12 tells us, "Whoever exalts himself will be humbled, and whoever humbles himself will be exalted." My fourth divorce was so devastating to me because I thought I had finally figured out how to have a successful marriage. I entered the relationship desiring to serve and to give, rather than to be served and to get. Nothing was wrong with my method of loving, but plenty was amiss with my motive for doing so.

I prayed that God's love would flow to me and through me, and it did in many and various ways, but the divorce revealed to me my relying upon my own fleshly, self-righteous energy more than on God's grace. My pride ignored James 1:17: "Every good and perfect gift is from above, coming down from the Father." And I ignored 1 Corinthians 4:7: "What do you have that you did not receive? If then you received it, why do you boast as if you did not receive it?" Here I was trying to earn a good gift from God by my efforts. I was living by law rather than by basking in God's grace.

The present engagement period is, therefore, a most necessary time to increasingly grow in knowing ourselves and also knowing our one, true love better. If you ask the average person to condense the character of God as depicted in the Old Testament, one might hear something along the lines of "just" or "wrathful." But the word that comes to my mind is *faithful*. God keeps his promises. He cannot lie. And he promises to love us forever with an unfailing, steadfast love. The Hebrew word is *hesed*. It is a limitless, loyal love full of compassion.

Hebrews 11:1 tells us, "Now faith is the assurance of things hoped for, the conviction of things not seen." Assurance. Conviction. Rare commodities—no, rather they are miracles—in a world that is broken by sin. I grew up hearing only two things are certain in life—death and taxes. That is not true. Our Beloved is the most certain thing in our lives. When he speaks, it shall be so. Read Genesis 1 quickly to yourself right now. Notice the repetition of "and God said . . . and it was so."

No one else in all creation can make such a consistent, constant claim. Not the best parent or spouse or friend or coworker. In their fallenness, they forget; they get sick; they die. In a broken world, they have accidents, they run late, they overschedule. In their flesh, they manipulate; they get revenge; they have moods. One of the greatest pains in our world is a broken promise. All of us have been on the receiving end, and all of us have been on the offending end of a broken promise. Neither position feels good. Neither position *is* good.

If we set our hopes and dreams on anything or anyone in this fallen world, we will be disappointed eventually. Good gifts from God cannot be God, despite how desperately our flesh want them to be. On the contrary, our Beloved is not like people or things in this world. He always delivers. He always comes through as we need. He speaks and it is so. Twenty-four hours a day, 100 percent of the time, guaranteed. No wonder why one of the most repeated words in the Bible is *amen*, "it shall be so." God will do what he says he will do. Period.

Marriage in this world has many purposes. It provides a place for righteous sexual expression. It provides an environment by which to raise children. It provides a relationship whereby faith in the Lord may grow. It provides companionship. It provides a way for needs to be met. It provides an avenue for love to flourish. It provides a partnership that loves and serves others.

But over and above and through all these purposes lies one overarching purpose that points to our heavenly Beloved like no other metaphor: marriage is a commitment, a covenant, to be with each other *come what may*. For sickness or health, for better or worse, for richer or poorer, till death parts them, spouses vow to stick together. This is why God hates divorce (Mal 2:16). It is not in his nature to abandon us. He keeps his commitment. He is faithful.

The engagement period is a time for trust in our Beloved to grow. It is a time for us to see that he really is for us, that he desires our good, and that he will do what he promises to do. Trust is even more important than understanding, for there will certainly be times when we do not understand what our Beloved is doing or why he is doing it. There will be maddening times when he is not doing what we think he should be doing. But to continue to trust that he is working for our good and that he is good is absolutely vital.

Now there are two senses in which we can talk about faith. The first sense, the subjective sense, is the amount of trust we have. In this focus the emphasis is on us and how much we trust. But the second sense, the objective sense, is the person or thing we trust. It is in that sense that we want to focus primarily in this chapter. For the more we grasp the object of our trust, our Beloved, and how trustworthy, loyal, and faithful he truly is, then the subjective sense will follow. Christians make a big mistake in confusing these two senses and in letting the first sense dominate in our thoughts and discussions on faith. But focusing on the object of our faith, our Beloved, can lead us to assurance, confidence, and hope. For it is the object of our faith, not the strength of our faith, that saves us. You might want to reread that last sentence.

Listen to what our Beloved says to us about his faithfulness:

"The Lord will fulfill his purpose for me."	Ps 138:8
"I am with you always."	Matt 28:20
"If we confess our sins, He is faithful and just to forgive us our sins and to cleanse us from all unrighteousness."	1 John 1:8–9
"Our Lord Jesus Christ, who will sustain you to the end, guiltless in the day of our Lord Jesus Christ. God is faithful."	1 Cor 1:8–9

"Now may the God of peace himself sanctify you completely, and may your whole spirit and soul and body be kept blameless at the coming of our Lord Jesus Christ. He who calls you is faithful; he will surely do it."	1 Thess 5:24
"But the Lord is faithful. He will establish you and guard you against the evil one."	2 Thess 3:3
"If we are faithless, he remains faithful—for he cannot deny himself."	2 Tim 2:13
"Let us hold fast the confession of our hope without wavering, for he who promised is faithful."	Heb 10:23
"I will never leave you or forsake you."	Heb 13:5
"Then I saw heaven opened, and behold, a white horse! The one sitting on it is called Faithful and True."	Rev 19:11

When we dwell on the subjective sense—how much trust we have—we inevitably end up in one of two places: pride or despair. For those moments or seasons in life when we feel our trust is quite strong, the temptation is to feel some pride in a false sense of accomplishment on our part. But for those moments or seasons in life when we feel our faith is quite weak and impotent, we can be tempted to despair and doubt if we actually have any kind of saving faith in us at all. Our enemy, the accuser, enjoys having us in either position, for then our eyes are on ourselves rather than on our Beloved.

Fortunately, our Beloved comes to our rescue in both circumstances. Listen carefully to Hebrews 12:1–2, 4: "Let us run with perseverance the race that is set before us, looking to Jesus, the founder and perfecter of our faith, who for the joy that was set before him endured the cross, despising its shame, and is seated at the right hand of the throne of God." Did you catch it? Jesus began and will complete our faith. What a relief! If left up to us, we would be most certainly lost and would lose faith. But God is faithful and will do what is necessary to craft enduring faith in us.

Romans 1:17 tells us, "The righteous live by faith." There is no other way in which we can possibly live in a broken world, separated from God by sin. Our Beloved had to walk by faith when he took on human flesh and lived among us. One of my frequent prayers has been "I believe; help my unbelief!" (Mark 9:24). Faith isn't natural for us. Doubt is natural, envy is natural, fear is natural, worry is natural. We need power from above to believe. We need to trust our Beloved. We need the gift of faith.

So, how do we get it? Romans 10:17 tells us, "Faith comes from hearing, and hearing through the word of Christ." Faith gradually grows through thousands of devotions, sermons, conversations, and Bible studies over our lifetime of being engaged. The gospel takes deeper root in our hearts and minds as we hear, read, and speak God's Word. We need to be reminded so often because we are so forgetful and so distracted. We need to contemplate often the trustworthy track record of our Beloved, because faith needs to be constantly fed.

Our forefathers in the Old Testament needed the same gift. I think one of the most frequent commands God gave them was "remember." They were to remember that God had delivered them from captivity in Egypt and that he was sending his Messiah to usher in his kingdom. It is not unlike the two major events we are to remember today, our being delivered from sin and death at the cross and Christ's return to take us to shalom in the new heavens and new earth. Furthermore, Old Testament believers would build piles of rocks called Ebenezers to mark any event when God's faithfulness was apparent. Then in the future, whenever they passed these markers, they would talk about God's faithfulness with their children in an effort to instill faith in them.

A later chapter will explore the 66 Love Letters our Beloved has given to us to build our faith in him. Another chapter will discuss the importance of getting to know his family, so we can taste and see that he is good (Ps 34:8). But for now, it is sufficient to remember that faith is one of the three greatest gifts we can receive (1 Cor 13:13). And our Beloved is the most faithful person we will ever know. As we shall see in the next chapter, his faithfulness gives us another gift that is also much needed to see us through this time of preparing and waiting for his return.

QUESTIONS FOR DISCUSSION/REFLECTION:

1. Which sense of faith do you catch yourself thinking about and talking about more, your level of trust OR the One you are trusting? What differences can you spot when you dwell on the subjective sense more than the objective sense?

2. Can you look back and see that faith has grown in your life? What has made it grow?

3. Pause and consider that everyone in your life at present, if you live long enough, will eventually leave you for some reason, but God won't. Thank him for his faithfulness to you.

4. Make a list of events and seasons in your life when God proved his faithfulness to you. Consider making a memory book of God's faithfulness in your life. Share your life story with others to show God's work of grace in it.

5. Sing or listen to "Great is Thy Faithfulness."

Chapter 5: **We Need the Gift of Hope**

ENGAGED PEOPLE LOVE TALKING and thinking about the future. They make plans. They share dreams. After teaching teenagers for over forty years, I can say with confidence that their favorite Bible passage is overwhelmingly Jeremiah 29:11. No wonder, as it speaks to the future yearnings of our heart, "For I know the plans I have for you, declares the Lord, plans for welfare and not for evil, to give you a future and a hope." The best is yet to come.

Being engaged broadens our horizons. It makes us think ahead like nothing else. It fills us with anticipation. We need to be careful, therefore, of limiting this Jeremiah 29 promise to only this world. Now that he has risen from the dead, our Beloved is certainly not limited by time or space and neither are we. His resurrection now gives us an eternal, rather than a temporal, perspective. Envision a nail hole that once held a picture on a wall. The hole represents your time of being engaged in this world; the wall represents your time of being married to your Beloved in the next world. We want to focus more on the marriage to come than on the engagement at present. For the best is yet to come.

Romans 8:24–25 gives us a definition of *hope*: "Now hope that is seen is not hope. For who hopes for what he sees? But if we hope for what we do not see, we wait for it with patience." Biblical hope is a future certainty. It is not mere wishful thinking. Hope will happen. We can bank on it. But it is not going to be here and now. It will be there and then, when our Beloved returns and ushers our new, resurrected, and glorified bodies into the new heavens and new earth with him. The best is yet to come.

I once heard that we should ask what we *really* want rather than simply, "What do I want?" The answer to the latter question usually comes from our flesh and is very nearsighted. The answer to the first question, complete with a qualifier, leads us to the inner man, to our deeper desire from our new heart. Sin has corrupted us so deeply that our flesh now sees evil as good and good as evil (Isa 5:20). Paul cautions against having fleshly nearsightedness in 1 Corinthians 15:19: "If in Christ we have hope in this life only, we are of all people most to be pitied."

I think most of our conscious hopes are relegated to this world. No wonder God tells us in Ephesians 3:20, "Now to him who is able to do far more abundantly than all that we ask or think." The time of engagement, therefore, is a time to ponder and desire the bigger picture. Therefore, it must be profitable, although a bit painful, to look for the deeper desires underneath our surface ones here. We need to look farther ahead than we normally do.

So, what do I *really* want? I want to feel totally secure, significant, and satisfied. I want to be accepted and delighted in. I want to know another and be known. I want perfect love, perfect peace, perfect joy, perfect performance, perfect relationship, perfect everything. I want no more tears, crying, mourning, or death. I want to be free of any detestable thoughts, words, or actions.

I want what all believers pray for in the Lord's Prayer: his kingdom to come and his will to be done. Indeed, we are members now of his kingdom and his will is being done, but the fullness of each is yet to be experienced in all its glory. A Day is coming where we will live in perfect righteousness and where every thought, word, and action will be in perfect alignment with God's will.

I want to be free of all negative feelings: fear, doubt, worry; sadness, grief, depression; guilt, shame, regret; anger, frustration, rage. I want to be free of feeling lonely. I want to be free of every kind of pain. I want to feel really good, almost euphoric, all the time. I want a world without sin or the effects of sin. I want to be with God. I want the garden of Eden before the fall. I desperately want something that can't be had . . . yet. I want to be married now. But I am only engaged now. The best is yet to come.

So, how can we now live without having what we really want? We need hope. How can we attain a certain hope for our eternal marriage with our Beloved? A first step is to acknowledge and feel the pain and disappointment surrounding everything in this world. There is a cosmic disappointment, a curse from the fall into sin, that infects everything and everyone that crosses our path. Nothing is perfect. No one is perfect. Nothing is completely fulfilling. Yet, we have a deep, deep desire for it to be so.

All delights in this world are appetizers; they are not the full, satisfying meal that is coming. The problem is when our rebellious, Old Adam nature tries to make a four-course meal out of hors d'oeuvres. They simply cannot do what they were not designed to do. They cannot fully satisfy our innate hunger for shalom, that state or condition where everything is precisely as it should be. This will be when everything and everyone are whole, united, and harmonious. The Greek idea of perfection was when something performed according to its design. I want perfection from myself and from everyone and everything around me. I suspect that you do too.

What is absolutely the worst thing that could possibly happen to us? There is only one correct answer: eternal separation from our Beloved, otherwise known as hell, where there is continual weeping and gnashing of teeth (Luke 13:28; Matt 13:42; Matt 8:12; Matt 24:51; Matt 25:30; Matt 22:13). This is the very thing that our Beloved has promised to protect us from. Therefore, the exact opposite, the absolutely best thing that could happen to us, is to spend eternity with him in the new heavens and new earth.

His 66 Love Letters remind us of this truth. Psalm 16:11 tells us, "In your presence is fullness of joy; at your right hand are pleasures forevermore." "The Lord is my shepherd; I shall not want" (Ps 23:1). "Seek first the kingdom of God and his righteousness, and all these things will be added to you" (Matt 6:33). With our Beloved comes everything else we deeply want. Job seemed to understand this by his words in Job 19:25–26: "For I know that my Redeemer lives, and at the last he will stand upon the earth. And after my skin has been thus destroyed, yet in my flesh I shall see God." His eyes were not on this world. He believed the best is yet to come.

Our Beloved also showed us how to live with hope. "Let us run with endurance the race that is set before us, looking to Jesus . . . who for the joy that was set before him endured the cross" (Heb 12:1–2). What was the joy set before Jesus? I believe it was twofold. First, I think he was looking forward to pleasing our Father by fulfilling his mission to rescue us. He was anticipating the joy of returning to the right hand of the Father in heaven and being in his presence once again. And secondly, I think he was anticipating the joy of our wedding and marriage with him.

Today you and I have a choice of where we fix our eyes. We can look to the present or to the past and sit with what is or with what might have been, or we can look to the future and rest with what will be. We can stare at the crosses in the race we have been running, or we can gaze at the joy set before us. The former will lead us to sorrow and despair; the latter will lead us to joy and hope. Our best day is ahead of us; it is not behind us or at present.

Having hope is vital, because I can say from personal experience that divorce often happens when at least one person loses hope in a relationship. It might be an oversimplification, but I also believe this is what leads many people to commit suicide. The gift of hope enables us to endure the engagement period of preparing and waiting and not give up. Our enemy can tempt us to doubt that God will not deliver what he has promised. Romans 8:32 is a good antidote to this temptation: "He who did not spare his own Son but gave him up for us all, how will he not also with him graciously give us all things?" God will not hold anything back, because he has already given us his best. Real, positive, out-of-this world change is coming.

Tim Keller, in speaking about "Uncovering Hope" to students at the University of Oxford, said, "What we believe about the future determines how we experience the present."[1] The world would have us believe that this is the only life we will ever live, and so we had better grab everything we can this minute. But Paul gives us a better hope in 2 Corinthians 4:8–9: "We are afflicted in every way, but not crushed; perplexed, but not driven to despair; persecuted, but not forsaken; struck down, but not destroyed." He could say this because he had his eyes on the resurrection, "knowing that he who raised the Lord Jesus will raise us also with Jesus and bring us with you into his presence" (2 Cor 4:14). For us believers, whatever happens to us in this world is the worst part of our existence that we will ever experience. But the best is yet to come.

God likens this present engagement period to our living in a wilderness (Rev 12:6). What can keep us going through droughts and hard times? Where do our minds go when our earthly tents are wasting away and health is deteriorating? Where do our minds go when relationships end and grief sets in? Where do our minds go when we are facing the ultimate and final enemy, death? Thanks to our Beloved and to our Father who raised him, the resurrection is *the* game changer. This life is not all there is to our existence; eternity awaits. Indeed, for us believers it has already begun with our engagement to our Beloved.

Lastly, remember how we defined biblical *hope* as "a future certainty"? Listen to Ephesians 2:4–6: "But God . . . made us alive together with Christ . . . and raised us up with him and seated us with him in the heavenly places in Christ Jesus." In a very real sense, we already have one

1. Keller, "Uncovering Hope."

foot in heaven today because that is where our Beloved is reigning on the throne right now. And where he is, there are we. Larry Crabb spoke to the significance of the two, ultimate, life-changing events in *Inside Out* when he wrote, "The joy we can know in this present world depends entirely on what the Lord Jesus has done and what He yet will do. Remove the cross and the second coming and every joy becomes an illusion."[2] Do you want more joy in your life? Contemplate what our Beloved did for us on the cross and that he will return to take us to the new earth we deeply desire. Stop trying to make this world paradise and start thinking more about the real paradise ahead. The best is yet to come.

At this point, it is probably easy to see how faith and hope are connected. God will deliver what he has promised because he is trustworthy. But 1 Corinthians 13:13 tells us that neither of these great gifts is the greatest in our gift registry. There is another item that will fill our new home with such joy and pleasure far beyond what we have experienced in this world. It is what we most deeply crave. It is that for which we were designed. It is, I believe, what quieted Job's questioning why he was suffering (Job 42:5–6). It is what every recipient of a miracle of Jesus experienced. It is what the thief on the cross heard (Luke 23:43). It is the most pervasive quality, I believe, that we will notice about our Beloved when we find ourselves in his presence.

To whet our appetites, perhaps it would be a good idea to stop reading this book right now, pour yourself a glass of wine, and read Song of Solomon before advancing to the next chapter.

> Draw me after you; let us run. The king has brought me into his chambers. We will exult and rejoice in you; we will extol your love more than wine; rightly do they love you. (Song 1:4)

> He brought me to the banqueting house, and his banner over me was love. Sustain me with raisins; refresh me with apples, for I am sick with love. His left hand is under my head, and his right hand embrace me! (Song 2:4-6)

It is finally time to talk about love.

---

2. Crabb, *Inside Out*, 229.

QUESTIONS FOR DISCUSSION/REFLECTION:

1. How often do you think about heaven or living with God in the new earth?

2. What do you think about when you think about heaven or living with God in the new earth?

3. What do you hope for in the next world that you have not been able to fully experience in this one?

4. The vast majority of your existence is ahead of you, not behind you. Your time in this world is a blip on the radar screen of eternity. The best is yet to come. How might these facts move you to live and relate differently now?

5. Sing or listen to "Be Still My Soul."

Chapter 6: **We Need the Gift of Love**

AFTER BEING DIVORCED SEVERAL times, I am now very much aware that what I want—no, what I *really* want—is not just love. I want unfailing, steadfast love. The unflinching, unwavering, unending kind. I want limitless, loyal love. I want perfect love, the kind that no weak, immature, broken human in this world can give me. I need someone out of this world. Praise God the Father for sending him!

The situation is complicated by the fact that I am not easy to love. I am, as they say today, high maintenance—very high maintenance. Most of us are. But we like to think we are otherwise. We like to think we are nice, lovable people, but we are actually quite self-absorbed, desperate, and demanding people. Fortunately for us, our Beloved came to save the sick and needy and poor in spirit. He lives to resurrect those who are dead. All praise, glory, and honor to him; our Beloved has perfect love that casts out all fear of our not being loved.

Paul tells us in 1 Corinthians 13 that love is the greatest of God's gifts. When I was younger, I was surprised that faith wasn't the greatest of the gifts. My self-righteous flesh might have been showing as I was focusing on what I must do in order to be saved. It can be tempting to put faith in our faith and see it as our work until we realize that our faith is very weak and, like everything else good in our lives, exists solely by the grace and Spirit of God. Love is also the essence of God's eternal character. It is who he is. And it will totally characterize the new earth. Selfishness and lawlessness enshroud earth at present; selflessness and righteousness will permeate the new earth.

C. S. Lewis defined agape love as "wishing and working for another's good, often at a cost to oneself."[1] Do you want to know what real love looks like? Look at Jesus on the cross. "In this is love, not that we have loved God but that he loved us and sent his Son to be the propitiation for our sins," John told his readers (1 John 4:10). A couple's love flows to them and through them and between them and out from them to God and to others. It all begins and is empowered by God's love for them. And God's love is "patient and kind; not envious or boastful; not arrogant or rude. It does not insist on its own way; it is not irritable or resentful; it does not rejoice at wrongdoing, but rejoices with the truth. It bears all things, believes all things, hopes all things, endures all things" (1 Cor 13:4–7). "Love never ends" (1 Cor 13:8).

Paul prayed for us in Ephesians 3:16–19 that "He may grant you to be strengthened with power through his Spirit in your inner being, so that Christ may dwell in your hearts through faith—that you, being rooted and grounded in love, may have strength to comprehend with all the saints what is the breadth and length and height and depth, and to know the love of Christ that surpasses knowledge, that you may be filled with all the fullness of God." Our love for God begins in time and continues in time and for eternity with his love for us. As we come to know ourselves better—especially how depraved and corrupted by sin we really are—the more incredible and amazing his love for us will appear. And our gratitude and love for him will grow.

I believe this is the heart of what the present engagement period for us is all about—to grow in the love of our Lord. It increases as we gaze upon and ponder and marvel at his tremendous love for us that took him out of the comfort and bliss of heaven to become a weak and dependent baby, to become a man of many sorrows, well acquainted with grief, that led to his willingly being beaten and going to the cross in our place, to pay our debt, to remove our guilt and condemnation, so he could please our Father and save our eternal souls so we could be one with him forever. "Greater love has no one than this, that someone lay down his life for his friends" (John 15:13). This is what he paid to be with us forever. This is the one to whom we are engaged. No wonder we need the Spirit to help us even grasp how great this love is.

Contemplate this. Jesus cried out in excruciating anguish on the cross, "My God, my God; why have You forsaken me?" (Matt 27:46). Is there a

---

1. Lewis, *Mere Christianity*, 129–130.

greater agony than the loss of a relationship we desperately want? If you have lost such a relationship, you can imagine somewhat the pain Jesus experienced in feeling the loss of his Father's presence on the cross. And, if you are a parent who has lost relationship with a child, then you can understand the Father's pain in watching his son die on that cross.

Every relationship in this broken world ends, either by death or by one party moving away from the other for a variety of reasons. This is not so with our Beloved. First Thessalonians 5:10 gives us an astounding truth: "Our Lord Jesus Christ, who died for us so that whether we are awake or asleep we might live with him." God loves us to, through, and beyond death. It is the reason he died for us, to pay the bride price for our eternal union and communion with him.

The engagement period is a time for us to see that everything God tells us in his 66 Love Letters is true. Nothing in all creation will be able to separate us from the love of God in Christ Jesus our Lord (Rom 8:39). He really does deliver us from all our troubles. He really never will leave us or forsake us (Heb 13:5). He really does abundantly pardon and forgive us (Isa 55:6). He really is close to the brokenhearted and saves those who are crushed in spirit (Ps 34:18).

In his book *Deeper*, Dane Ortlund writes, "The deepest destiny of your life is to descend ever deeper, with quiet yet ever-increasing intensity, into the endless love of God . . . We grow in Christ as we go deeper into, rather than moving on from, the verdict of acquittal that got us into Christ in the first place . . . Our growth in Christ will go no farther than our settledness, way down deep in our heart, that God loves us. And he loves us simply because he is love and he chooses to love us."[2] How settled are you, deep in your heart, that God loves you? If there is any question, I suspect you might be looking at your circumstances or yourself too much. Focus instead on the cross, and remember that God has taken care of your biggest problem: sin and separation from him.

We celebrate at Christmas and Easter that the Father loved the world so much that he sent his only son to rescue us. Jesus left the comfort, safety, warmth, and blessedness of being in the Father's presence to come to this dark, cold, violent world of sin and be separated from the Father. As a man, he would experience all of what we experience. Our pain and suffering become his. He walked where we walk, in a world of death and decay, of deceit and doubt. He suffered and was tempted just as we are. It was love that

2. Ortlund, *Deeper*, 83, 85.

brought him here to live and to die so that we can marry and live with him forever, free of any more pain and tears and suffering and death.

When the Spirit empowers us to grasp his great love for us, then we are transformed by the same Spirit to move toward loving God and loving others. "So we have come to know and to believe the love that God has for us. God is love, and whoever abides in love abides in God, and God abides in him. By this is love perfected with us, so that we may have confidence for the day of judgment because, as he is, so also are we in this world . . . we love because he first loved us" (1 John 4:16–17, 19). His return for us will be the happiest day of our existence.

Jesus condensed the Ten Commandments into two: love God and love others. Luther once said, "God gets up every morning and milks the cows."[3] God loves people through people. Contemplate how many people God has loved you through so far today. How many hands were involved in supplying all your food needs, from production to distribution? How many hands were involved in your transportation today? Don't forget the strangers driving next to you safely, obediently following traffic laws. How many hands were involved in building the house or apartment in which you live? How many people maintain it? How many people made your clothing? It is no small thing for people to simply show up and do their job on a daily basis. It is called "common grace," and it all comes from our very loving, gracious Beloved.

The engagement period is a time for us to walk as he walked in this world. Ephesians 2:10 says, "For we are his workmanship, created in Christ Jesus for good works, which God prepared beforehand, that we should walk in them." So, now we can love others the way he loves us. We, too, can love sacrificially. We can give, expecting and getting nothing in return. The engagement period is a time for being restored as the loving creatures we were made and redeemed to be. Life with our Beloved and his family in the new earth will be characterized by pure love. It will be a place where we will love God supremely and each other perfectly. In the meantime, there is fruitful labor for us to do. This is the truest and best benchmark of our preparation for the wedding: are we loving God more and others better? We won't experience perfection in this world, but God's love will certainly move us in this direction.

Jesus raised the bar for sin and for love. His Sermon on the Mount in Matthew 5—7 takes murder and moves us beyond actually taking another's

3. Moulds, "Key Reformation Themes."

life unjustly to having hate in our heart. He does the same with adultery; it is not only the act of sex outside marriage, but it is also looking lustfully at another. And he also raises love to new heights. "The old commandment is the word that you have heard. At the same time, it is a new commandment that I am writing to you" (1 John 2:7–8). God has always wanted us to love others. The original command was to love our neighbor as we love our-selves (Matt 22:29). But now in Christ we are called to "love one another as I have loved you" (John 15:12). To lay down our life for someone is another level of love! And that is the adventurous life our Beloved is calling and empowering us to live with him (1 John 3:16).

Because I am old and have taught for four decades, many see me as wise. I always wince a bit when I hear the compliment. First, I know that much wisdom comes from having lived foolishly. But secondly, I would much prefer that others see me as loving. Sadly, my love has often been corrupted. Like the Romans, I have been judgmental. Like the Corinthi-ans, I have been proud. Like the Galatians, I have been legalistic. Like John's readers of his letters, I have been licentious. Like the Colossians, I have been hindered by the earthly clothes of sexual immorality, idolatry, anger, wrath, malice, and slander. I must know his love and forgiveness for me if I am to love at all. His love must simply flow through me, as I cannot create it on my own.

Sin dehumanizes us. It turns us inward. But the love of our Beloved makes us human again. It turns us outward toward him and toward others. Just think of when others praise or thank us for doing something good for them. It feels really good, doesn't it? Sometimes it can bring us to tears. It touches something deep in our soul. We were created to love. Then sin killed our ability to love. But now we have been saved by love, lavished with love, indwelt by love, so we can love. We have been born again. Our Beloved invites us to a life of love with him now and continuing into eternity.

Engagement life with him now in this world, however, entails some big surprises. Our Beloved is very strong, very good, and very loving all the time. Note "*all* the time." Therefore, the three greatest gifts of faith, hope, and love are experienced by us and developed in us in a most shocking and unexpected manner. We contemplate in awe and wonder how he delivers these and many other good gifts to us next.

QUESTIONS FOR DISCUSSION/REFLECTION:

1. Love "bears all things and endures all things." List all the things God bears and endures with you.

2. Someone once said you can tell how much a person loves you by how much they are willing to suffer for you. Who could possibly come close to loving you the way God does? Think about it and thank him for what he has suffered for you.

3. Are you more assured that God loves you today than you were ten years ago? If "yes," why? What has happened to give you more confidence in his love?

4. Do you love God more today than you did ten years ago? Do you love others better today than you did ten years ago? What evidence would you point to for both answers? If "yes" to either question, what changed you?

5. Sing or listen to "What Wondrous Love Is This."

Chapter 7: **We Have a Gift Registry**

I KNOW OF ONE primary method by which we can acquire faith, hope, love and all the gifts we need to transform us to become the bride we are going to be in our eternal marriage. These gifts are priceless and necessary for us to live now and later in the kingdom of God. Hebrews 5:8 tells us the stunning manner in which they will be acquired: "Although he was a son, he learned obedience through what he suffered." Engagement is a time for us to grow up in him, to become like him, through the gift registry of suffering. Think about it.

Scripture describes the bride we are to be as holy, sharing the righteousness of our Beloved. Hebrews 12 says what God lovingly uses to develop such quality in us is painful discipline. Romans 5 tells us that endurance, character, and hope are produced in us through suffering. Hebrews 2:10 tells us that Jesus was made perfect through suffering. James 1:2–4 tells us, "Count it all joy, my brothers, when you meet trials of various kinds, for you know that the testing of your faith produces steadfastness. And let steadfastness have its full effect, that you may be perfect and complete, lacking in nothing."

Colossians 3 says we are to be people who set our minds on things above and not on things that are on the earth. I can think of nothing that helps us detach and become disenchanted with things of this world more than the cosmic pain and disappointment that is embedded in everything. Everything. It takes time to discover this and find these gifts from our Beloved in and around tears and mourning. The painful length of our engagement, for example, is a gift in itself. Picture our heavenly lover having a specially designed calendar and checklist just for us. The wedding will not occur until all the preparations in us, for us, for him, have been completed.

To be sure, our flesh wants to avoid sanctification and jump to glorification. We want to skip the engagement, fly to Vegas, and get married now. We want a victorious Christian life with nothing but success, health, and happiness. But it can't be done. Not where we currently reside. Not in our present condition. Our Beloved walked where we walk. He carried not only our transgressions and iniquities to the cross but also our infirmities and sorrows (Isa 53:4). We are therefore not immune from any trouble, heartache, or failure. They only serve to make us increasingly more dependent upon our Beloved. And more like him.

We must discover that our Beloved is superior to anything and anyone. Jesus is our best parent. Jesus is our best friend. Jesus is our best spouse. Jesus is our best thrill, pleasure, joy, excitement, peace, love, life. And he is our righteousness. We have none of our own. This becomes all the more apparent by every grief, heartache, and sin we experience in this broken world. C. S. Lewis said, "If I find in myself a desire which no experience in this world can satisfy, the most probable explanation is that I was made for another world."[1] We can read about this, and we can be told this. But we need to discover for ourselves via experiencing the reality of it. This is one redemptive reason for our tears in this world. "By mere words a servant is not disciplined, for though he understands, he will not respond" (Prov 29:19). Suffering, more than any other method of education, leads us to change how we think and how we behave. This is why parents spank toddlers and ground teenagers.

Paul likened many of God's gifts to clothing. He told the Colossians to put on compassion, kindness, humility, meekness, patience, and forgiveness (Col 3:12–13). From personal experience and the testimony of other believers, I believe these qualities are most deeply fashioned in the cauldron of affliction. If I am brutally honest, I must admit that what most needs changing in my life is not my circumstances or another person. It is me. And I am very stubborn and entrenched in my self-absorbed ways. Once God rescues us, his major goal is then to renew us to be conformed to the image of Jesus.

And what is Jesus like? He loves our Father supremely and others sacrificially. He depends totally on our Father, and he knows this world is passing away. At any given point in time prior to my death, I will need to love God more and others better. I will need to be hoping more for things in the next world than for anything in this one. And our faithful and

---

1. Lewis, *Mere Christianity*, 136–37.

powerful God will use everything to work toward this good. This includes pain, suffering, and failure.

Psalm 1 tells us, "Blessed is the man . . . whose delight is in the law of the Lord . . . in all that he does he prospers." Martin Luther explains how this can be true: "Beware that prosperity is not understood as prosperity of the flesh. This prosperity is hidden. If you do not hold fast to it in faith, you might rather call it the greatest adversity . . . For what is more wonderful than that the believers increase when they are destroyed, that they multiply when they are diminished, that they overcome when they are subdued, that they are victorious when they are defeated? Thus, God exalts his saints, that the height of misfortune becomes the height of prosperity."[2] It seems paradoxical, but—thanks be to God—we gain, and perhaps especially so, when we lose.

One of the most comforting passages in Scripture for us believers is Romans 8:28–29: "And we know that for those who love God all things work together for good . . . to be conformed to the image of his Son." Our Beloved turns "all things" into good for us. Our sin, our failures, our foolishness, others' sin against us, tragedies that naturally befall people in a fallen, cursed world. God uses all things to mold and shape us to become increasingly like our Beloved. And I suspect that much of the transformation happens on the inside, in our hearts and minds. We become a little more compassionate, more empathetic, more humble, more forgiving, more grateful, more Christ-centered. If the Lord is removing our idols from us, where does that action primarily take place? In our heart. God moves us to become more loving toward and dependent upon him.

The gifts for us in the registry of suffering are of the cross and not of glory in this world. A theology of the cross maintains that God has revealed himself most fully and significantly in the suffering, death, and resurrection of Jesus. God's power is most clearly seen in the "weakness" of the cross; God's wisdom is most clearly seen in the "foolishness" of the cross (1 Cor 1:18). The trials and tribulations in our lives are thus illuminated with great meaning when seen through the lens of the cross of our Beloved. Moments of difficulty are used to complete the good work he has begun in us. "My grace is sufficient for you, for my power is made perfect in weakness," Jesus told Paul in 2 Corinthians 12:9. He is working in and through those trials. He uses our weaknesses, hardships, persecutions and calamities to demonstrate his power, grace, mercy, love, and glory.

2. *Lutheran Study Bible*, 847.

Trials drive us to pray and to read the 66 Love Letters more frequently and intensely than we normally would without them. They help us set our minds on things that are above, in our future, forever home with our Beloved, rather than on things that are on earth, where everything is temporary and decaying. They help us trust in our Beloved with all our heart rather than trust in our reason or understanding or success (Prov 3:5). The wonderful gifts of this personally designed registry of suffering lead us increasingly to see that our life is hidden with Christ in God and nowhere else. Our Beloved is the greatest gift in the registry. He is our "wisdom from God, righteousness and sanctification and redemption" (1 Cor 1:30).

The flaming darts of the evil one lead us to return again and again to our only source of help and strength, to our Beloved. He alone can give us unending grace, mercy, forgiveness, patience, and love. There is a popular expression used by well-intentioned but uninformed believers to comfort another in pain. "God will never give you more than you can handle." This expression is not biblical. The opposite is true as seen in 2 Corinthians 1:8–9: "For we were so utterly burdened beyond our strength that we despaired of life itself. Indeed, we felt that we had received the sentence of death. But that was to make us rely not on our ourselves but on God who raises the dead." Nothing moves us more quickly to fly into the arms of our Beloved than to be in over our head in a difficult circumstance.

Our enemy wants us to believe the lie that our Beloved does not actually love us, that he doesn't care, and that he can't be trusted. But our Beloved is the only one who loves us with the kind of unfailing, steadfast love we deeply crave. This is the only love that will be with us to, through, and beyond death. It is only fully discovered, however, in the pains and heartaches of this world. Every death, divorce, rejection, abandonment, abuse, betrayal, accident, illness, and misfortune is the Amazon truck driving the fruit of the Spirit to our door. There is no other way to acquire love, joy, peace, patience, kindness, goodness, faithfulness, gentleness, and self-control (Gal 5:22–23).

Finally, the gift registry of suffering gives us a solidarity and unity with Jesus. Our life of trials and tribulations is walking as our Beloved walked and becoming a partner, a companion, a spouse like him who is well acquainted with grief. And, at the same time, he is walking with us in our shoes, experiencing what we are experiencing. He knows us intimately. He knows a word before it is on our lips (Ps 139:4). He gathers our tears in a bottle and counts our tossing and turning in our sleep (Ps 56:8). My experiences in life show me that nothing cements a close relationship better than enduring a trial together. Psalm 34:18 assures us, "The Lord is near to the brokenhearted and saves the crushed in spirit."

No one can better sympathize, empathize, and understand the pains we endure than Jesus. He was intensely tempted with pride, greed, and lust (Matt 4). He suffered the death of a close family member (Joseph) and a friend (Lazarus). He was misunderstood, abandoned, and betrayed by close friends. He was not attractive by worldly standards (Isa 53:2). He was estranged from siblings who believed he was crazy and a blight to the family name (Mark 3:21). He had no wealth or possessions but lived day to day (Matt 8:20). Religious and government leaders hated him and plotted to kill him. He was physically and verbally abused. He was beaten mercilessly. He felt forsaken by God. He experienced death.

Therefore, we also pick up our cross and have our own Gethsemane experience. We pray earnestly that the marriage be saved, the infirmity be healed, the disaster be avoided. But like our Beloved, we pray ultimately not for our will to be done but for his will to be done. We come to value his kingdom over our kingdom and his presence over his presents. We wait expectantly for our Beloved yet again to turn something very bad into something very good, to demonstrate his power in weakness and hardship, to turn darkness into light (Ps 18:28).

Revelation 21:2 says, "And I saw New Jerusalem coming down from heaven as a bride prepared for her husband." When did the Spirit prepare the church as a bride? During the tribulation in the end times right before Jesus returned for her. Similarly, God prepared his Old Testament people for the promised land by delivering them through plagues and forty years of wilderness wandering. C. S. Lewis said, "We are not necessarily doubting that God will do the best for us; we are wondering how painful his best will turn out to be."[3] Renovation implies a tearing down and a building up. God seems to do two primary works in the lives of nations and individuals: he humbles and he exalts (Matt 23:12). God disciplines those whom he loves (Heb 12:6). We see it in the histories of Israel, Joseph, David, Paul, and others. And we see it in our own lives.

Dietrich Bonhoeffer, at the end of his classic *The Cost of Discipleship*, writes,

---

3. Lewis, *Collected Letters*, 285.

If we would have a share in that glory and radiance, we must first be conformed to the image of the Suffering Servant who was obedient to the death of the cross. If we would bear the image of his glory, we must first bear the image of his shame. There is no other way to recover the image we lost through the Fall.

To be conformed to the image of Christ is not an ideal to be striven after. It is not as though we had to imitate him as well as we could. We cannot transform ourselves into his image; it is rather the form of Christ which seeks to be formed in us (Galatians 4:19) and to be manifested in us . . . We too must bear the sins and sorrows of others . . . The Christian life is a life of crucifixion (Galatians 2:19). (Our) life is marked by a daily dying in the war between the flesh and the spirit, and in the mortal agony the devil inflicts upon (us) day by day. This is the suffering of Christ which all his disciples on earth must undergo.

This is what we mean when we speak of Christ dwelling in our hearts. His life on earth is not finished yet, for he continues to live in the lives of his followers. Indeed, it is wrong to speak of the Christian life: we should speak rather of Christ living in us (Galatians 2:20, Philippians 1:21). And because He really lives his life in us, we too can walk even as He walked (I John 2:6), do as He has done (John 13:15), love as He has loved (Ephesians 5:2), and forgive as He forgave (Colossians 3:13).[4]

The two become one. It is happening as you read this. Indeed, it is a present fact but not yet a blessed experience as it one day will be. As the transformation is occurring, something else amazing is simultaneously taking place, according to 2 Corinthians 4:17: "For this light momentary affliction is preparing for us an eternal weight of glory beyond all comparison." Paul alludes to the future benefit that results from this world's trials in his first letter to Timothy: "For while bodily training is of some value, godliness is of value in every way, as it holds promise for the present life and also for the life to come" (1 Tim 4:8). The gift registry of suffering in this world is storing up gifts for us beyond our imagination in the next world. Our engagement pains are making the marriage joys all the greater.

But until we are experiencing those glorious joys, we have the lengthy gift registry of suffering to endure. There will be many, many times when we will need reassurance of our Beloved's love for us, his goodness, and his power to work for good in all things for our sake and for his purposes. There will be many, many times when we will need to lift our eyes off the

4. Bonhoeffer, *Cost of Discipleship*, 301–304.

gift registry and onto the giver and the life he has planned for us. It will be in such times that we can run to and open a most precious gift that he has given to us for here and now. Nothing will calm our fears and soothe our anxieties more than hearing the voice and truths of our Beloved in his 66 Love Letters.

QUESTIONS FOR DISCUSSION/REFLECTION:

1. What trials and times of suffering have you experienced in this world?

2. Can you now see how God used those times to transform you to be more like Jesus? How specifically has God changed you for the better through suffering?

3. Read 2 Corinthians 12:7–10. What does God use in our lives to show his power? Note why God gave Paul a thorn. Are their times in your life when he might have done the same thing for you for the same reason?

4. Read Hebrews 12:5–14 and 2 Corinthians 4:16–18. What do these passages tell you about difficult times in your life?

5. Sing or listen to "It Is Well With My Soul."

Chapter 8: **We Have 66 Love Letters**

I REMEMBER VIVIDLY THAT during my first engagement I couldn't wait to get home to call my fiancée. It was joyous to talk about our days together and our plans for our wedding and life beyond. I lived on the East Coast, and she was in the Midwest, so there was a two-hour time gap. More than once, I fell asleep before saying "good night." Have you ever fallen asleep while praying to our Beloved? I am not sure that is a bad thing.

Communication is important in any relationship. I think there is a close correlation between frequent and clear communication and a close and strong relationship. People in love, for example, enjoy talking together for hours. Our Beloved has given us 66 Love Letters that we get to read and reread and reread to see his heart and know his mind. He gives us just the right word when we need to hear it. His Word enlivens, mends, heals, and inspires. It convicts, forgives, comforts, and motivates. With our Beloved, there are no elephants in the room that go ignored. "No creature is hidden from his sight, but all are naked and exposed to the eyes of him to whom we must give account" (Heb 4:13). There are no times when we get the silent treatment due to a mood, illness, distraction, busyness, lack of forgiveness, or exhaustion.

We often read the Bible as a series of disconnected stories, each with a moral for how we should live our lives. Such a view misses the relationship and connection with our Beloved. It is not primarily a handbook for how we can do this or that to have a successful life. Rather, it comprises a single story, telling us how the human race has gone wrong and how God through Jesus Christ has come to rescue us and will return to put things right. It is a book by and about our Beloved. John 5:39 confirms this: "You search the Scriptures because you think that in them you have eternal life;

and it is they that bear witness about me." The Bible shows us Jesus, the one who is our life. Even those paragraphs and pages that are difficult or challenging to read and understand ultimately point to the Father's salvation plan fulfilled in Jesus.

Our sinful flesh has tainted how we see our Beloved. Our enemy, the liar, wants to show us a very contrary picture of God. We are tempted to make him in our image or in the image according to the world. We need the Word of Truth to transform us by the renewal of our minds. His 66 Love Letters help us increasingly see him as he is: loving, trustworthy, pure, good, wise, just, merciful. He came to save us not to condemn us. We therefore not only want to love him more than we love anything or anyone else, but we also want his will to be done.

The Word of our Beloved has several things to say about itself and our relationship with him.

"My soul longs for your salvation; I hope in your word."	Ps 119:81
"I wait for the Lord, my soul waits, and in his word I hope."	Ps 130:5
"Your words were found and I ate them, and your words became to me a joy and the delight of my heart, for I am called by your name, O Lord, God of hosts."	Jer 15:16
"Man shall not live by bread alone, but by every word that comes from the mouth of God."	Matt 4:4
"Blessed rather are those who hear the word of God and keep it!"	Luke 11:28
"Truly, truly I say to you, whoever hears my word and believes him who sent me has eternal life."	John 5:24
"If you abide in my word, you are truly my disciples, and you will know the truth, and the truth will set you free."	John 8:31b–32
"If anyone hears my words and does not keep them, I do not judge him; for I did not come to judge the world but to save the world. The one who rejects me and does not receive my words has a judge; the word that I have spoken will judge him on the last day."	John 12:47–48
"If anyone loves me, he will keep my word, and my Father will love him, and we will come to him and make our home with him."	John 14:23

"Sanctify them in the truth; your word is truth."	John 17:17–18
"Let the word of Christ dwell in you richly, teaching and admonishing one another in all wisdom, singing psalms and hymns and spiritual songs, with thankfulness in your hearts to God."	Col 3:16
" . . . when you received the word of God, which you heard from us, you accepted it not as the word of men but as what it really is, the word of God, which is at work in you believers."	1 Thess 2:13
"Of his own will he brought us forth by the word of truth, that we should be a kind of first fruits of his creatures."	Jas 1:18
" . . . you have been born again, not of perishable seed but of imperishable, through the living and abiding word of God; for 'All flesh is like grass and all its glory like the flower of grass. The grass withers, and the flower falls, but the word of the Lord remains forever.' And this word is the good news that was preached to you."	1 Pet 1:23–25

Our Beloved's 66 Love Letters have power. Romans 10:17 tells us, "Faith comes from hearing, and hearing through the word of Christ." Our trust and love for our Beloved grows as we get to know him better. Isaiah 55:11 tells us that God's Word "does not return to me empty, but it shall accomplish that which I purpose and shall succeed in the thing for which I sent it." Hebrews 4:12 says, "The Word of God is living and active, sharper than any two-edged sword, piercing to the division of soul and of spirit, of joints and marrow, and discerning the thoughts and intentions of the heart." Reading the Bible, therefore, is a highly personal and relational experience. Community with our Beloved is formed and continued through such communication. He is pouring his life into us. We often speak of studying the Bible, but the Word is also studying us, sizing up where we are and what we need. And we always need him.

I do not know where I would be today without my Beloved's 66 Love Letters. By his grace and Spirit, I cherish them. God has given me the ability to remember so many precious passages. Frequently in my life I heard them read or taught and it was precisely what I needed to hear. Sometimes they warned me; sometimes they chastised me; sometimes they comforted me. But they always pointed me to my Beloved and to his unfailing, steadfast love and forgiveness for me. They moved my eyes away from myself and onto him. And that gave me the energy to keep going through whatever circumstances surrounded me.

In *Gentle and Lowly* Dane Ortlund describes why we need to read and hear them over and over again: "It takes a lot of sermons and a lot of suffering to believe that God's deepest heart is 'merciful and gracious, slow to anger.' The fall in Genesis 3 not only sent us into condemnation and exile. The fall also entrenched in our minds dark thoughts of God, thoughts that are only dug out over multiple exposures to the Gospel over many years."[1] If you have ever wondered why we keep hearing the same old message in church, this is why. We need to hear it repeatedly because we have layers and layers of misconceptions and falsehoods that need to be revealed and discarded so the truth can illuminate our minds and hearts. No one knows upon which number of times of hearing or reading the Word the light will go on and we will see more of reality, more of ourselves, more of our circumstances, more of him.

The 66 Love Letters tell us to think about "whatever is true, whatever is honorable, whatever is just, whatever is pure, whatever is lovely, whatever is commendable, if there is any excellence, if there is anything worthy of praise" (Phil 4:8). The 66 Love Letters are the testimony of God's grace in the gospel. That is ultimately Jesus. Have you ever considered that he is the best thought we will ever have? He is also the most glorious beauty we will ever see. But at present we must settle for his voice. Thus, I find it most calming and soothing to read from the 66 Love Letters early in the morning and right before bedtime.

Lovers bundle and keep love letters. They give life and hope every time they are read. They keep the fires of love burning in hearts. How much more powerful are the words from our Beloved. They change our heart, our mind, and our spirit. They reveal how we are not like our Beloved, how far we fall short of his character, and how much our Beloved forgives and loves us anyway. The world, the accuser, and our conscience continually shove our sinfulness and sins in our face. They want us to look at our former bank account and see nothing but our former debt and poverty. But the 66 Love Letters show us our Savior and Redeemer and riches in him.

The Bible reminds us that our betrothal to our Beloved is now legally binding. We now have a joint account. Paul tells us, "So you also must consider (count) yourselves dead to sin and alive to God in Christ Jesus" (Rom 6:11). Our new account is overflowing with his abundant wealth. Jesus has

---

1. Ortlund, *Gentle and Lowly*, 151.

paid for our sin and its damages. "There is therefore now no condemnation for those who are in Christ Jesus. For the law of the Spirit of life has set you free in Christ Jesus from the law of sin and death. For God has done what the law, weakened by the flesh, could not do" (Rom 8:1–3). We need not fear Judgment Day for we have already been judged and acquitted in Christ.

In our fight against sin, the incessant suffering all believers face, the 66 Love Letters are the sword of the Spirit. When we are bloodied, wounded, and despairing in the battle, our Lord's Word reminds us that we have the strength of the Lord. We now wear the armor of our Beloved. We have his truth, his righteousness, his peace, his salvation covering and protecting us (Eph 6:10–17). The 66 Love Letters remind us we have a new identity, new power, and new destiny. And they remind us, despite feelings or appearances to the contrary, that our Beloved is loving, forgiving, and in control.

Finally, the 66 Love Letters fuel our communication with our Beloved. They prompt us to respond. The book of Psalms actually puts words to our prayers. It is, after all, the prayer book of our Beloved. No Old Testament book is quoted more often by Jesus or by the New Testament writers than Psalms. Don't know what to pray? Read through the Psalms until you find your prayer for today.

The constant reading and hearing of our Beloved's love story for us, accumulated over decades, ignites a desire within us for a life change. "God is working in us both to will and to work for his good pleasure" (Phil 2:13). We want to put down our script and take up his. We want to more actively and willingly participate in the story he is writing. We now want to live for him rather than for ourselves. We now want to follow him. We sense we are being moved by the author and perfecter of our faith from slavery to freedom. The Word is accomplishing what our Beloved intends for us—oneness with him. We are becoming a submissive bride.

QUESTIONS FOR DISCUSSION/REFLECTION:

1. How often do you read or hear God's Word? What effect has it had on you?

2. What biblical books have been most meaningful to you? Why? What particular passages have been most meaningful to you? Why?

3. What teachers/authors/speakers have been most influential for you in your understanding of Scripture? How so?

4. Read Hebrews 4:12–13. God's Word reveals who we are and who God is. At this point in time, who do you understand yourself to be, and who do you understand God to be?

5. Sing or listen to "Thy Strong Word."

Chapter 9: **We Want to Submit**

BEFORE WE GOT ENGAGED, we did whatever we wanted, when we wanted, and how we wanted. Being single affords us much freedom and autonomy. But engagement changes all that. We now think of someone else when we make decisions. It is a way to give our Beloved glory, which means "weight." We consider his name and how our plans will impact his reputation. We consider his kingdom and his will. We actually want that above our kingdom and our will. We can pray "thy will be done" and mean it from the new heart, new spirit, and the Holy Spirit in us.

It is not a popular word in this fallen world with rebellious people who want to be their own god, but the word *submit* needs to be embraced here. It literally means to "send under." The question then becomes "what exactly do we send under our Beloved?" I believe it is our will, wishes, and desires. I believe it is our very lives. The ultimate act of submission was seen in Gethsemane, when Jesus prayed, "My Father, if this cannot pass unless I drink it, your will be done" (Matt 26:42). Our Beloved husband submitted all his will under the Father's and came to this world, died, and rose again for the sake of us, his chosen bride. It is only appropriate that we now do the same. With his Spirit in us, we are now both called and desire to be like our Beloved.

But changing from wanting God's will over and above our will is not easy. In fact, it is impossible for us to do. The rebellious, self-absorbed spirit must die in us so that something new can come alive. The battleground for this transformation is in our heart and mind. It begins before we get out of bed. Clambering for our attention, thoughts, plans, duties, obligations, and concerns rush at us immediately upon our waking up. As C. S. Lewis wrote in *Mere Christianity*, "And the first job each morning consists simply in shoving them all back; in listening to that other voice, taking that other point of view, letting that other larger, stronger, quieter life come flowing in. And so on, all day long. Standing back from all your natural fussings and frettings."[1] We choose to think about our Beloved and what he would do and how he would do it. We consult his 66 Love Letters to see his desires and thoughts. And that exercise leads us to pray.

The prayer our Beloved taught us begins with him. It is not about us. It is about his kingdom, his will, and his glory. The engagement period is a time in which we will progressively move from being self-centered to God-centered. This is no small transformation! Old habits and patterns are hard to break. But, if I am completely honest, my situation is much worse than a bad habit. It is an inborn disposition, a hardened mindset, of believing I know what is best. Adam and Eve ate of the tree of knowledge of good and evil. Now I am prone to call "evil good and good evil, to put darkness for light and light for darkness . . . I am wise in my own eyes" (Isa 5:20–21). I am hardwired to rely on my own understanding and subsequently of wanting my own way. Being engaged starts to dismantle my rebellious and foolish independence.

Thanks to God's grace, we now want to see as our Beloved sees. Sin has distorted how we see God, ourselves, others, and circumstances. "The eye is the lamp of the body. So, if your eye is healthy, your whole body will be full of light, but if your eye is bad, your whole body will be full of darkness" (Matt 6:22–23). Being engaged to our Beloved changes our perspective on everything. We know that he is the way, the truth, and the life (John 14:6). We now want to hate what he hates and love what he loves. We want his mind and to think what he thinks. We want to see his perspective on everything. This is a crucial aspect of submitting to him.

My sinful flesh all too easily insists on my own way, leans on my own understanding, and seeks my own happiness. Following it always leads eventually to pain, shame, and guilt. This is the very time I feel most distant from my Beloved. I am a stubborn and independent fiancée. At those times he gently and patiently comes to me and helps me see what is true. He reminds me that my way leads to death, but his way leads to life. He reminds me that what once was mine is now his and what was his is now mine. It is such an understatement to say we married "up." Theologians call it the "great exchange."

---

1. Lewis, *Mere Christianity*, 198.

Our Beloved takes upon himself what we have to offer—sin, guilt, condemnation, debt, and death—and he gives us what he has to offer—righteousness, forgiveness, salvation, freedom, and life. It is so humbling to realize that we bring something actually worse to the table than nothing. We bring bankruptcy and a death sentence. But our precious Beloved accepts the exchange willingly! What wondrous love is this, o my soul?! Think about it: he left the glory of heaven to take on human flesh. He gave up his freedom and autonomy. He put himself in a position to hurt, cry, suffer, and die. Why? So he could complete his Father's mission to rescue us and so be united with us now and for eternity.

Second Corinthians 5:14–15 tells us, "For the love of Christ controls us, because we have concluded this: that one has died for all, therefore all have died; and he died for all, that those who live might no longer live for themselves but for him who for their sake died and was raised." This is no small change! We are hardwired in the flesh to live for ourselves. The default mechanism inside us is set for me, me, me, my, mine, mine. We come out of the womb demanding our name be hallowed, our kingdom to come, and our will be done. But "the love of Christ" now controls us. Our submission begins with our grasping his submission. It changes everything about us: how we think, how we speak, and how we act. It reorients our entire worldview, our purpose, our goals.

Thanks to the Spirit in us, we now increasingly want to please the Beloved. We will even sacrifice our freedom, our independence, our pleasure, for the sake of his. Like the old hymn, we sing from our heart: "Take my life and let it be consecrated, Lord, to Thee."[2] We realize that everything we have and are have been given to us by him to be used in his service for the praise of his glory. By his grace and Spirit, "I delight in the law of God, in my inner being" (Rom 7:22). Now I want what he knows is good and avoid what he knows is evil, for he sees truth much better than I. My sin nature has made me blind and foolish. I know following my passions and desires will lead to death but following him will lead to life.

Fortunately, he meets us where we are. Where we go, he is there. Where he is, there are we. What else do the words from Matthew 28:20 mean: "I am with you always, until the end of the age"? And the words from Ephesians 2:6: "Raised us up with him and seated us with him in the heavenly places in Christ Jesus"? We now get to say "our Father," and we pray in the name of our Beloved. Thanks to his blood that forgives us, we

---

2. *Lutheran Hymnal*, 59.

are "holy, without blemish, and above reproach before him" (Col 1:22). "He made him to be sin who knew no sin, so that in him we might become the righteousness of God" (1 Cor 5:21). Wow, wow, and wow!

Now whatever happens in our life—during this engagement period—is to be seen in the larger context of our Beloved and us. That is always the bigger story going on, our relationship with our Beloved, above, around, through, and in every event that comes our way. The smaller story is our divorce, our accident, our health, our finances, our relationships. It is at such times it is most helpful to remember to submit. Focus in faith on what God is doing. Luther maintained that our Beloved is always up to something. Romans 8:28–29 assures us what that something ultimately is—conforming us more and more to the likeness of our Beloved. He is making us new. So, we submit to his loving care. We want him to have his way with us.

Furthermore, let us not forget that we now have a joint account with our Beloved. What is his is now ours, but what is ours is now also his. Our health is his. Our relationships are his. Our possessions are his. Every dollar, not just what we give to charities or the church, is his. Titus 2:13–14 reminds us, "Our great God and Savior Jesus Christ, who gave himself for us to redeem us from all lawlessness and to purify for himself a people for his own possession." Every aspect of our lives is now at his disposal, to be used for his kingdom purposes and to prepare us for our marriage with him.

Paul told Timothy about a joint investment we now have in 1 Timothy 4:8: "For while bodily training is of some value, godliness is of value in every way, as it holds promise for the present life and also for the life to come." Paul told the Romans, "For the creation waits with eager longing for the revealing of the sons of God" as the creation itself is waiting "to be set free from its bondage to corruption and obtain the freedom of the glory of the children of God" (Rom 8:19, 21). The transformation that God is doing in us now will show up in the new earth. Submitting to God's will and ways is freedom and wealth. We who once fell short of his glory will one day share it completely. But for now, the process of increasing submission to the will of our Beloved will be like being in labor pains, both for those around us and for ourselves (Gal 4:19).

The engagement period is not only a time to help us submit to *what* our Beloved does but also to *how* he does it. To our reason he should simply act in worldly power to accomplish things. For example, when Jesus came to earth the first time, people expected and wanted an earthly king. They longed for a return to the glory days of David and Solomon, when Israel was the number one power—politically, economically, and militarily—in the world. Instead, the Messiah defeated sin, death, and satan by being falsely accused, beaten, dying on a cross and rising again. Similarly, he invites his followers to take up their cross and follow him (Matt 16:24).

So, our Beloved mysteriously and marvelously works through our crosses, our weaknesses, and hardships. His power is demonstrated most clearly at such times (2 Cor 12:9–10). The worldly victory and success we crave may not be the route he uses to lead us through the race marked out for us (Heb 12:1). He uses the most unlikely of conditions to accomplish his purposes and our good. And Jesus has become to us "wisdom, righteousness, sanctification, and redemption" (1 Cor 1:30). He, not our performance or our wonderful circumstances, is our victorious life. In the final analysis, we need only one thing, and praise God, we have him (Luke 10:42).

If we think about it, we really do want to submit everything to our Beloved. His earthly brother wrote, "God opposes the proud, but gives grace to the humble. Submit yourselves therefore to God" (Jas 4:6–7). Peter, who probably understands humility better than most, wrote, "Humble yourselves under the mighty hand of God so that at the proper time he may exalt you" (1 Pet 5:6). Earlier in that letter he had encouraged wives to "let your adorning be the hidden person of the heart with the imperishable beauty of a gentle and quiet spirit, which in God's sight is very precious. For this is how the holy women who hoped in God used to adorn themselves, by submitting to their own husbands" (1 Pet 3:4–5). Godly people submit to God.

Our inborn fleshly pride, however, is the chief barrier to our submitting. Pride is the anti-grace state of mind. It thinks in terms of having earned and achieved something. Pride has a sense of entitlement. It thinks, "I did A, so of course I should have B." Pride is competitive and wants more than what another has. It thinks, "Because I did such and such, I am better than so and so." C. S. Lewis called it the greatest sin and described how we can detect it: "Whenever we find that our religious life is making us feel that we are good—above all, that we are better than someone—I think we may be sure that we are being acted on, not by God, but by the devil. The real test of being in the presence of God is that you either forget about yourself altogether or see yourself as a small, dirty object. It is better to forget about yourself altogether."[3]

---

3. Lewis, *Mere Christianity*, 124–125.

The real diabolical kind of pride leads us to judge God. We want to steal glory from our Beloved. We forget our role as bride and assume his place. We judge how he is ruling his universe and our small part of it. We become critical because he is not doing what we believe he should be doing. We forget, "The earth is the Lord's and everything in it. The earth is the Lord's and everyone in it" (Ps 24:1). He is God; we are not.

Finally, how we make decisions may reveal our submissiveness as much as the decisions themselves. What is our attitude? Do we have a demanding spirit? Are we being dependent on him? Are we trusting him? Are we seeking his thoughts on the matter? David understood that his efforts were in vain if the Lord were not with him. David wanted to move in accordance with God's will. In 2 Samuel 2:1 we read, "David inquired of the Lord, 'Shall I go up into any of the cities of Judah?' And the Lord said to him, 'Go up.' David said, 'To which shall I go up?' And he said, 'To Hebron.' So David went up there." Let this be our mindset the rest of our days before making a decision: "I need to discuss this with my Beloved first." It might help to check with other family members to see what he would like. We can reread his 66 Love Letters. But we ultimately pray and desire what Jesus did in the Garden of Gethsemane: "Not my will but Thy will be done" (Matt 26:39).

There is much talk today in education and business about leadership and being leaders in the world, but we forget that we are all ultimately followers. We should frequently ask ourselves, "Whom am I following?" One of the saddest experiences I have as a Christian teacher is when I discover that a former student is no longer walking with the Lord. Without exception, I have observed that these people are no longer hanging around God's Word or God's people. On the contrary, they are listening to and trusting another voice, another authority. The dictionary defines *authority* as "a power to influence or command thought, opinion, or behavior."[4] We all must listen and submit to some authority. For Christians, we have concluded with Peter, "Lord, to whom shall we go? You have the words of eternal life" (John 6:68). Our Beloved does everything for the Father's glory and for our good. He gave himself up for us (Eph 5:25). This is the person we really want to follow.

How do we know if we have begun to submit to him? Our submitting to our Beloved is a result of being made alive with Christ (Eph 2:5). In his book *Ephesians*, Darrell Johnson says the signs of submission are not difficult to detect:

---

4. *Merriam-Webster English Dictionary* (1996), s.v. "authority."

1. We love Christ and want to love him more;

2. we love his Word and want to understand and live it more;

3. we love his family the church despite their blemishes and brokenness;

4. we love the world and want others to know him; and

5. we long for his return not only for the world's healing but also because we finally will see his face.[5]

I suggest there is one more sign that we are submitting to God. It is in a humble approach to how we live life. We acknowledge and trust his ultimate control. The flesh has an arrogant presumption: we control more than we actually do. The flesh deceives us into believing we have godlike powers. James described it this way: "Come now, you who say, 'Today or tomorrow we will go into such and such a town and spend a year there and trade and make a profit' . . . Instead you ought to say, 'If the Lord wills, we will live and do this or that" (Jas 4:13–15). Humility recognizes that God controls the universe with his sovereign will. Nothing happens unless he allows it to happen. We are not in control. He is. And in our more sane moments, we really don't want it any other way.

Following our Lord and submitting to him will never be perfect in this fallen fleshly earth suit; our flesh makes us all control freaks. Submitting is a big part of our being sanctified. It is our Beloved's movement in us, directing our mind, heart, and attitude toward increasingly deferring to him and to his control. The process feels like an ongoing, nonstop tug of war. Just when it appears we have made some progress, we discover another part of life where we need to release our grip and let go. Therefore, we need one more gift daily in abundance to endure the engagement period.

QUESTIONS FOR DISCUSSION/REFLECTION:

1. What areas of your life are hardest to completely submit to God's will? What present situations or decisions in your life have you yet to discuss with your Beloved? Stop and do that right now.

2. Read Colossians 1:13–23. Everything—including you—was made by, for, and through Jesus. What are the implications therefore for your life and everything in it?

5. Johnson, *Ephesians*, 130—131.

3. What is your controlling compass that steers how you make decisions today? In other words, what is your end goal that you have in mind? Has that changed in your life? If "yes," when and why did it change, and what had been your goal?

4. Looking back, how did living for yourself rather than for God cause problems in your life? When and how has God humbled you?

5. Sing or listen to "Take My Life and Let It Be."

Chapter 10: **We Need Ongoing Forgiveness**

BECAUSE WE STILL WEAR this Old Adam earth suit, our submission to our Beloved's will is not perfect in this world. Therefore, we need ongoing forgiveness if our relationship is to survive. I believe most divorces occur because of an unresolved conflict. There is a line with a box to check on a divorce decree that reads "irreconcilable differences." In my experience, that difference or conflict centered around a very highly emotional issue for my wife or for me. The conflict occurred in what one of us believed was a nonnegotiable, deal-breaker area. It was such an emotional minefield that it paralyzed us from being able to have the necessary conversations and internal commitment to resolve it.

Sin is a much bigger problem than we often realize. Paul gives us the grim picture in Romans 7:19–21: "For I do not do the good I want, but the evil I do not want is what I keep on doing. Now if I do what I do not want, it is no longer I who do it, but sin that dwells within me. So I find it to be a law that when I want to do right, evil lies close at hand." I believe it is the sheer grace of God that the world in which we presently inhabit is not worse. Sometimes I marvel that there are not more car accidents, murders, rapes, thefts, suicides, divorces, and wars. It is his great grace that as many relationships in families, churches, the workplace, and the state operate as smoothly as they do. Sin—any sin—is crouching at the door for each one of us.

I once heard that reconciling is much more important than resolving. I think there are some situations in this broken world that are too tangled and crooked to be made straight or to be resolved. Unresolved conflict over an idol though eventually eats away at whatever had originally bonded the two parties, and it prevents any meaningful efforts of reconciliation. The conflict is excruciatingly painful for the idolater—it feels like death—and gradually fear takes over and hope is lost. When that happens, the relationship is usually ended by the one who has the deeper sense of fear or hopelessness.

The two areas that seem to be the center of much conflict in an earthly marriage are children and money. I have also seen sex, family, and careers be divisive forces between spouses. When one understands idolatry, divorce becomes more understandable. Idolatry is very often the reason we do anything wrong. There is something we believe we must have to feel satisfied or secure or significant. It is very much like an addiction. That something reveals itself to be more important to our heart than our spouse or even God himself.

We have been chosen to leave, cleave, and be one flesh with our Lord and Savior. Some counselors believe that most divorces are caused by one or both spouses not fully leaving whatever they clung to formerly for their security, significance, and satisfaction. It is too tempting to return to former foundations, to Egypt if you will, when times get difficult and challenging in this wilderness. And they will. Our Beloved warned us they would.

I suspect this is the biggest reason why subsequent marriages have an increasingly lower percentage of success. There simply is less bonding adhesive to keep two previously married spouses together with new spouses. We are hard wired in our fallen flesh to bond to something, to someone, to give us a sense of well-being and homeostasis. I am afraid we therefore more resemble Gomer, Hosea's repeatedly unfaithful wife, than we resemble Ruth, the daughter-in-law who faithfully stood by her mother-in-law Naomi. Luther seems to agree:

> Uncleanness remains in him (a believer) to keep him humble, so that in his humility the grace and blessing of Christ taste sweet to him. Thus, such uncleanness and such remnants of sin are not a hindrance but a great advantage to the godly. For the more aware they are of their weakness and sin, the more they take refuge in Christ.[1]

Our ongoing need for forgiveness, therefore, drives us to bond with our Beloved. So, what needs to grow in this time of engagement? Our dependence. Our complete and utter dependence on the grace, mercy, and forgiveness of our Beloved. Frankly, Jesus is the only one holding our relationship together. No one else is like him. Nowhere else will we find

---

1. Luther, "Commentary on Galatians," 5:19.

his grace, mercy, compassion, patience, and forgiveness. He is slow to anger and abounding in steadfast love. He is faithful, especially when we are unfaithful. In fact, our unfaithfulness and our unrighteousness only serve to demonstrate his faithfulness and his righteousness (Rom 3:5). His goodness and purity shine brighter next to our corruption and darkness. And our love and gratitude for him grow in the soil of our deep humility amid our failure and his forgiveness. As Luke 7:47 says, "He who is forgiven little, loves little."

We cannot find a more forgiving person in the universe than our Beloved. He is not like broken people in this world. Psalm 27:10 says, "For my father and my mother have forsaken me, but the Lord will take me in." His ongoing, daily forgiveness keeps our relationship together. And he forgives all kind of sin—sins of premeditation, sins of ignorance, and sins of weakness. He forgives our guilt, our rebellion, and our violation of his law even if we are unaware of it. This aspect of the Beloved was especially driven home for me as I prepared for a chapel a few years ago.

I was trying to find some way to visualize for the audience God's forgiving nature. I was teaching on Exodus 34:6–7, where God describes himself to Moses, "The Lord, the Lord, a God merciful and gracious, slow to anger and abounding in steadfast love and faithfulness, keeping steadfast love for thousands, forgiving iniquity and transgression and sin, but who will by no means clear the guilty, visiting the iniquity of the fathers on the children and the children's children to the third and fourth generation." I created a PowerPoint slide showing four generations of my family, where divorce is all over the family tree. I noted that we often see this aspect as pretty harsh on God's part, for sin to trickle down to children and grandchildren.

But then I noticed a footnote in my Bible for "keeping steadfast love for thousands." "Thousands" can also read "thousands of generations."[2] To show God's love and forgiveness to only one thousand generations, putting four generations on one slide, would mean I would have to make two hundred and fifty slides. I calculated it would take three to four hours simply to flip through that many slides! God's forgiveness simply dwarfs his punishment and justice and the curse of sin! No wonder James 2:13 urges us to show that "mercy triumphs over judgment."

Isaiah 55:7–8 also tells us how forgiving our Beloved is: "Let him return to the Lord, that he may have compassion on him, and to our God, for he will abundantly pardon. For my thoughts are not your thoughts,

2. *Lutheran Study Bible*, 154.

neither are your ways my ways, declares the Lord." Did you catch that? God is not like us judgmental people. He "abundantly pardons." First John 2:1 assures us, "But if anyone does sin, we have an advocate with the Father, Jesus Christ the righteous." Can you envision what our Beloved says to the Father? "He is trusting my righteousness, not his own." "She believes her debt has been paid by my blood." Praise God that he is our defender and daily declares our justification—"There is now no condemnation for those who are in Christ (Rom 8:1)"—otherwise, our relationship with him would be doomed.

There is, in the final analysis, only one irreconcilable difference, only one unforgivable sin that can divorce us from our Beloved. It is our believing one of two lies around our Beloved's forgiving us: 1) either we believe we do not need his forgiveness, or 2) we believe he can't or won't forgive us.

The rich young ruler is an example of the first false belief (Matt 19:16–22). You might recall he asked Jesus what he must do in order to be saved. Listen to this exchange: "And Jesus said, 'You shall not murder. You shall not commit adultery. You shall not steal. You shall not bear false witness, honor your father and mother, and you shall love your neighbor as yourself.' The young man said to him, 'All these I have kept. What do I still lack?'" Rather than telling the young man he has not kept the law perfectly and needs forgiveness—which probably would have been met with self-justifying arguing—Jesus shows him, "If you would be perfect, go, sell what you possess and give to the poor, and you will have treasure in heaven.' When the young man heard this, he went away sorrowful, for he had great possessions."

Judas is an example of the second false belief (Matt 27:1–5). Judas judged himself after realizing he had sinned by betraying innocent blood. He killed himself in futile despair. His heart condemned him and, unfortunately, he did not believe that "God is greater than our heart" (1 John 3:20). In other words, God's judgment of forgiveness, not condemnation, in Christ is greater than the law that accuses us.

Believing either lie—that I don't need forgiveness or that God can't or won't forgive me—separates us from the glue that bonds us together with our Beloved, the blood of Jesus poured out for our sinfulness and sins on the cross. We often discover things by contrast. Once we are engaged, it becomes clearer that it is foolish and futile to love something or someone that cannot love us with the unfailing, steadfast love we crave. Yet, our fallen flesh returns again and again to leaky wells, wells that cannot hold life-sustaining water to satisfy our thirsty souls.

Paul knew the awful dilemma we are now in. He wrote in Romans 7:18–20, "For I have the desire to do what is right, but not the ability to carry it out. For I do not do the good I want, but the evil I do not want is what I keep on doing. Now if I do what I do not want, it is no longer I who do it, but sin that dwells within me." We need a wedding when we will shed this body of sin and put on new clothes without spot or stain. But at present we are not yet wearing our wedding attire—we are only engaged, and therefore we constantly need daily forgiveness. As the engagement time goes on, we see more and more of our debt of sin and more and more of how much our Beloved paid for us. And his amazing grace becomes increasingly more amazing to us.

Luther's first of his *Ninety-five Theses* states that the life of a Christian is one of continual repentance. Consider the word *confess*. It means "to agree with." When we confess our sins, we agree with our Beloved that we have missed the mark; we have not lived as our Father designed us to live; we have not loved as Jesus loves; we have fallen short of his glory. In addition, we agree that we deserve his temporal and eternal punishment of death. But we don't stop there. We also confess or agree with God that we are now forgiven, that for the sake of Jesus we are not condemned. And we confess and agree with God that we wish to turn from lawlessness and live as he lives in righteousness. All three aspects of confession lead us to focus on our Beloved.

Titus 2:14 reminds us that Jesus "gave himself for us to redeem us from all lawlessness and to purify for himself a people for his own possession who are zealous for good works." This is a very difficult part of our engagement. We are unable to fully love our Beloved. We long to be like him, to love the Father most, and to love others as ourselves. We "delight in the law of God, in our inner being, but we see in our members another law waging war against the law of our mind and making us captive to the law of sin that dwells in our members. Wretched people that we are! Who will deliver us from this body of death? Thanks be to God through Jesus Christ our Lord!" (Rom 7:22–25).

The suffering process of sin-confess-turn, sin-confess-turn is accompanied by these flaming darts from the enemy. How many more times will God forgive me? When will God lose his patience and leave me? Why does he remain with someone so weak, so imperfect, so unfaithful to him?

These lies are so tempting to believe about our Beloved because we have probably experienced another human who has written us off, who has rejected us and ended relationship with us. We intuitively know that every human in this world has a line that we better not cross, or else we will face their abandonment and rejection.

This is when the most important part of the engagement period comes to play. It is absolutely vital that we increasingly get to know our Lord and lover well enough to see just how holy, how different, he is from anyone else we know. Hebrews 4:15–16 comforts us with these words: "For we do not have a high priest who is unable to sympathize with our weaknesses, but one who in every respect has been tempted as we are, yet without sin. Let us then with confidence draw near to the throne of grace, that we may receive mercy and find grace to help in time of need." He not only understands our weaknesses and our temptations, but he also sympathizes with us over them. He, too, was tempted "in every respect" as we are.

First John 1:7–9 gives the whole reason any one of us will ever make it to the wedding and the eternal marriage one day: "The blood of Jesus his Son cleanses us from all sin. If we say we have no sin, we deceive ourselves, and the truth is not in us. If we confess our sins, he is faithful and just to forgive us our sins and to cleanse us from all unrighteousness." Listen to the words we just read: "he sympathizes with our weaknesses; the blood of Jesus cleanses us; he is faithful; he will forgive us and cleanse us." If he urged his followers to forgive others "seventy times seven" (Matt 18:22), we know that our Beloved is a very forgiving person. "A contrite heart," one seeking his forgiveness, "he will not despise" (Ps 51:17).

If our Beloved ever stopped forgiving or showing us mercy, our relationship with him would be over because we have constant need for both. Fortunately for us, his love and mercy endure forever. We may not act or even feel perfect once we say "yes" to Christ. We have a new identity in Christ as his beloved, but we are not perfectly glorified in this world. When we Christians suffer—and our greatest and constant suffering is fighting our own sin—we do so in solidarity with Christ. We struggle together in a community of brokenness with other believers. Our shared hope is in a Savior whose body was broken for us and whose blood was shed for us.

I suspect many people today have an idealized vision of what their marriage should be in this world. I think many believe that the presence of conflict is automatically a bad thing. But one of the best wedding sermons I have ever heard—and, thanks to being a teacher of young people for over forty-six years, I have attended quite a few weddings—I heard this from my dear friend and mentor, Russ Moulds:

> Marriage seems like a pretty weighty responsibility to take on. Those unfamiliar with the gospel might think they've just heard a work order for some flawless, trouble-free, picture-perfect relationship—no conflict, no problems, no dirty socks, overdrawn checkbooks, and caps left off the toothpaste tube. But nothing could be farther from the truth. In fact, that kind of relationship would fail as a Christian marriage. A Christian marriage must have trouble and conflict in order to fulfill its purpose.
>
> You see, a Christian marriage refers to Christ and the church, not to some human ideal of wedded bliss. And how is it with Christ and the church? It's about sin and grace. It's about conflict and reconciliation. It's about failure and forgiveness. Both of these together are what people need to see but rarely do. The sin and conflict and failure are a given. There's no mystery about that. But a oneness sustained by the grace and reconciliation and forgiveness of Christ . . . now that is a mystery and truly a miracle. That's the very purpose of God in Christ.[3]

God's mercy and forgiveness that endure forever is indeed a mystery and a miracle. Our debt that we owe God is so astronomical that we can never calculate the total. Yet, our Beloved has paid the full price of our penalty with his blood. Our slate is wiped clean. Furthermore, we can now reckon, or do the math, and count ourselves righteous as he is righteous for we now, by his covenant of marriage, have his wealthy possessions credited to our name. We no longer have any liabilities; we now have only his assets.

I was asked recently what the most important lesson I have learned in my life of almost seven decades in this world. I think it is something that I continue to learn and relearn as time goes on. Today I am more certain of two things than I have ever been: I need a Savior and, thanks be to God, I have One. In other words, I need forgiveness and, thanks be to God in Jesus Christ my Lord, I have it. And so do you.

QUESTIONS FOR DISCUSSION/REFLECTION:

1. Have you ever been tempted to believe that God either can't or won't forgive you? What were the circumstances?

3. Dr. Russ Moulds's homily at wedding of Marty Schmidt (June 28, 1992).

2. Has your battle against sin led you to see yourself as a wretched person as Paul did in Romans 7:24? How often do you hear God's Word of absolution for you?

3. How often do you ask others for their forgiveness? To whom could you do this today?

4. Read Ephesians 4:32. To whom do you need to forgive today?

5. Sing or listen to "Jesus Paid It All."

Chapter 11: **We Join His Family**

IN THE FIRST CENTURY the betrothed husband would return to his father's house after the proposal and begin work on adding a room to the house. When the father determined that work was sufficiently completed, the son would then return for his bride, the wedding celebration would begin, and the two would begin living together in the father's house. The home usually included the extended family, father, mother, siblings, grandparents, and even servants and their families. To say that getting married to our Beloved is a family affair is an understatement. His relatives come from every tribe, language, and nation (Dan 7:13–14).

In Matthew 12:46–50 we read where Jesus recognizes this greater reality, his eternal family of faith: "While he was still speaking to the people, behold, his mother and his brothers stood outside, asking to speak to him. But he replied to the man who told him, 'Who is my mother, and who are my brothers?' And stretching out his hand toward his disciples, he said, 'Here are my mother and my brothers! For whoever does the will of my Father in heaven is my brother and sister and mother.'" Doing the will or the work of the Father is to believe in the one whom he has sent to save us (John 6:29). "He has delivered us from the domain of darkness and transferred us to the kingdom of his beloved Son" (Col 1:13).

Family dynamics, however, in God's family in a broken world, during the engagement period, can be quite messy and at times dysfunctional. We quickly discover that our new family members resemble us. Despite our occasional proud perspectives to the contrary, we are actually very similar. Every relative we meet reminds us of us: weak, immature, and broken. We are all incomplete works of God's pottery, in the process of becoming finished and whole, but with parts that still need to be removed, smoothed, or added (Isa 64:8). Interactions with these new people can be awkward and frustrating, with some uncomfortable and unsettling situations. Paul likened it to being in the pains of childbirth until Christ was formed in some of his spiritual children (Gal 4:19). Frustrations and conflicts, therefore, are inevitable.

The enemy will tempt us to remain isolated from the family of God. Pride, guilt, shame, and simply protecting ourselves from the uncomfortable can be rationalizations to remain distant. It can be less of a hassle to live as a single believer and mistakenly believe that our relationship with our Beloved is a private and individual matter. It is not. The writer to Hebrews told our relatives two thousand years ago, "We should not be giving up meeting together, as some are in the habit of doing, but encouraging one another—and all the more as you see the Day approaching" (Heb 10:25). The family of God is a gift to encourage each other. The Day, of course, is referring to our wedding, and it is much closer than it was two thousand years ago!

Because of our in-progress condition, it is most helpful to remember daily the ongoing forgiveness our Beloved lavishes upon us, so we can share it with other family members. Perhaps the family motto should be Ephesians 4:32: "Be kind to one another, tenderhearted, forgiving one another, as God in Christ forgave you." Indeed, notice what Jesus calls peacemakers in Matthew 5:9: "Blessed are the peacemakers, for they shall be called sons of God." It is worth noting that, in the first appearance Jesus made to his disciples after he rose from the dead, he gave them this charge, "'As the Father has sent me, even so I am sending you.' And when he had said this, he breathed on them and said to them, 'Receive the Holy Spirit. If you forgive the sins of any, they are forgiven them; if you withhold forgiveness from any it is withheld'" (John 20:21–23). Bear in mind the Father sent Jesus not to condemn the world but to save it (John 3:17). Likewise, Jesus has not sent us to condemn anyone but rather to proclaim the way of salvation.

The family of God, therefore, is the fellowship of the forgiven and the forgiving. It is comprised of people who, by God's grace and Spirit, know their desperate daily need for his ongoing forgiveness. They gather often and hear, sing, and taste the forgiveness of God through the shed blood and broken body of our Beloved. They battle the temptation of the enemy toward being legalists—people who try to live by the law but become critical condemners—or toward being licentious—people who complacently condone sin in the distorted name of "love." They meet regularly, bruised and battered, in their fight against the sinful flesh, the devil, and the world. The only antidote, the only salve, the only cure, is the ongoing proclamation of the forgiveness of sins in Christ. This is how they fulfill their royal priesthood role to anyone caught in any sin: they restore them gently by announcing sins are forgiven in Christ (1 Pet 2:9; Gal 6:1).

Amazingly, our Beloved's family, in all its dysfunction and immaturity, is called the body of Christ. Matthew 18:20 tells us, "For where two or three are gathered in my name, there am I among them." Jesus is our common denominator. He is the reason we are a member of his family and are able to relate with each other. Paul echoes the value of Christian fellowship in his words to the Romans: "I long to see you, that I may impart to you some spiritual gift to strengthen you, that is, that we may be mutually encouraged by each other's faith" (Rom 1:11–12). The family of God is his vehicle by which he overcomes the kingdom of darkness by the proclamation of the gospel. He is walking among us (Rev 2:1) and is using us weak vessels to bring people into his family and to restore them to his image.

Among the more mature members in the family of God, there is expressed a wonderful sense of grace. Worldly families are often plagued with judgment and condemnation. They divide into good sheep and black sheep, often in a fleshly attempt to justify themselves. Whereas the same can also be true for weak believers, more mature believers do not think they are superior to anyone, nor do they feel they are inferior to anyone. They believe they are "those who have obtained a faith of equal standing with (the apostles) by the righteousness of our God and Savior Jesus Christ" (2 Pet 1:1). Comparing ourselves with other family members becomes needless and, in fact, redundant when we realize we are comparing the righteousness of Jesus with the righteousness of Jesus. None of us have any righteousness of our own based on our doing any works of law.

In addition, we all are running our own race that is set before us (Heb 12:1). We have different circumstances and environmental influences. God's common grace blesses some with functional families or sound health or plentiful finances. But everyone eventually experiences some kind of pain and deficit. Some have this trial or that heartache. Conversing with Jesus at the end of the Gospel of John, Peter discovered that it is not helpful to compare our journey with that of other believers. "When Peter saw (John), he said to Jesus, 'Lord, what about this man?' Jesus said to him, 'If it is my will that he remain until I come, what is that to you? You follow me!'" (John 21:21–22). Our focus is to be on following our Beloved in the race marked out for us. Paul exhorted the readers of I Thessalonians 4:11, "Aspire to live quietly, and to mind your own affairs."

Ultimately, the body of Christ does not exist for its own sake. Indeed, if the entire world were Christian, we still would not have utopia or heaven, due to the sinful flesh in each of us. Rather, the body of Christ connects us to God. Being separated from our Beloved during the engagement season is not easy, but hearing his 66 Love Letters and being with his family give us a strong sense of his presence. Contrary to our usual feelings, he is with us, among us, and in us. This reality is most palpable when we gather with family to pray, sing, worship, and serve. A brother or sister becomes Jesus with skin on when we are blessed with their listening ear, encouraging word, forgiving heart, humble confession, or servant act. Indeed, Paul described it this way to the Corinthians: "For we are the aroma of Christ to God among those who are being saved" (2 Cor 2:15).

And while we do not always feel or experience our unity with other family members, it is indeed a fact. "There is one body and one Spirit—just as you were called to the one hope that belongs to your call—one Lord, one faith, one baptism, one God and Father of all, who is over all and through all and in all" (Eph 4:4–6). The full glory of God's family, just like our sinless individual glory, will be revealed at the wedding. Until then, we should expect some moments of uneasiness, awkwardness, disappointment, conflict, and even estrangement. But, on the other hand, we will also experience much more in common with our Beloved's family than we have with anyone who has chosen allegiance with the world. In fact, because we have been chosen out of the world, many non-family members will hate us. Remember they hated our Beloved (John 15:18–19).

I have been blessed to have been part of some strong Christian communities. God's grace has given me favor at four Christian high schools over the course of my life, and he has planted me in many strong, biblical churches with faithful pastors. When people have asked me what those communities were like, the best I could say was this: "The fruit of the Spirit is palpable there." Indeed, by the Spirit's moving in his people, the family of God exhibits love, joy, peace, patience, kindness, goodness, faithfulness, gentleness, and self-control (Gal 5:22–23). Believers love fellow believers in the family of God. They lay down their lives for each other (1 John 3:16). They share their gifts with those who do not have such gifts. The church is where we find nourishment and strength in the Word and in the sacraments of baptism and communion for this long engagement period of preparing and waiting.

The family of God has been entrusted with the most powerful, life-changing force in the world—the gospel. The gospel is the good news that God in Jesus Christ has taken care of our biggest problem, our sin that results in eternal death and separation from him. Our Beloved served out our death sentence, paid our debt, and appeased God's justful wrath. My mother liked to remind me that the world does not revolve around me. We will occasionally hear celebrities say that their family keeps them grounded. I think they are echoing Romans 12:3: "I say to everyone among you not to think of himself more highly than he ought to think, but to think with sober judgment."

Satan, this world, and our flesh can too easily lull us into a sense of entitlement. We can be tempted to believe that we deserve a happy family, obedient, respectful children, a good career, comfortable finances, loyal friends, and good health. But God's family, and in particular the preaching and hearing of the gospel, keeps us grounded. The gospel reminds us that we do not deserve a single thing beyond eternal death and damnation. The gospel reminds us that the good life is our salvation in our Beloved's atoning sacrifice for us. The disciples were reminded of this by Jesus: "Do not rejoice in this, that the spirits are subject to you, but rejoice that your names are written in heaven" (Luke 10:20).

It is a tremendous blessing to be part of the body of Christ. It is as close as we can come to being with our Beloved until we see his face. Spending time with his family is how we come to know and understand him better. It is there where we hear his childhood stories. It is there where we hear about his many exploits. It is there where we learn why he is the way he is. Our time with the family is vital, therefore, as it puts us in contact with the Trinity. And what is the Trinity like? Tim Keller expresses it this way in *The Reason for God*: "Each person of the Trinity loves, adores, defers to, and rejoices in the others. That creates a pulsating dance of joy and love. The early leaders of the Greek church had a word for this—*perichoresis*. Notice our word 'choreography' within it. It means literally 'to dance or flow around.'"[1]

So, picture what is happening in God's renewal work in the church today. We are all learning to dance and flow around him rather than around ourselves. God's sacrificial love is the music, and he has inserted himself within us. Our Beloved asks us to follow his lead. He serves rather than

---

1. Keller, *Reason for God*, 215.

focusing on being served. He gives rather than takes. He does his job and defers honor and attention to others. Because of sin that weighs us down, however, we frequently step on each other's toes and stumble. It is inevitable if we are around each other long enough. We insist on leading, demand our own way, and become out of step with our Beloved and, therefore, with other relatives. The Spirit, however, is the new rhythm of God inside us, and he is muting our predisposition to orbit ourselves and moving us instead to flow around our Beloved. He is piping into our head and heart God's song of love. And he is moving our feet to follow our Beloved's leading.

Our future marriage will have nothing but flawless dancing and moving in rhythm with our Beloved and with others. This is our hope. And it can help us experience the present in proper perspective. We can be thankful for moments of smooth flowing when it occurs as we mutually give to each other. And we can be forgiving when others have those moments of selfish, demanding leading in the dance rather than following the needs and concerns of others. The Spirit gives each of us gifts by which we are to use to build up others in the body of Christ (1 Cor 12:7).

As I write this, I am sadly aware that every relationship I have had in my seven decades has been marred and defiled somehow with selfishness. Our motives are always mixed due to our self-absorbed flesh clinging to us. I have all too often danced to my own tune and not to the song of the Beloved. But the family of God is being renewed to become better dancers. While Dr. Martin Luther King, Jr. was referring to the plight of black Americans, I believe his quote also captures quite nicely the plight of all Christians: "We ain't what we oughta be. We ain't what we want to be. We ain't what we gonna be. But, thank God, we ain't what we was."[2] This changes how we view ourselves and each other. We are works in progress. We are rehearsing for the eternal performance. Indeed, we are working out our salvation with fear and trembling, and God is working in us—giving us both the will and the work—for his good pleasure (Phil 2:12–13).

Paul said, "From now on, therefore, we regard no one according to the flesh . . . if anyone is in Christ, he is a new creation. The old has passed away; behold, the new has come" (2 Cor 5:16–17). When we get to our new home, we are all going to love each other perfectly. Brothers and sisters in Christ will love each other without defilement or corruption in the new earth much better than we ever could have in this world, despite what our relationship might have been (husband/wife, parent/child, friend, etc.). Now, by God's

2. King, "Dr. Martin Luther King, Jr.'s 1962 Speech."

grace, there are times we love each other very, very well. We dance uninterrupted a bit longer without stumbling or stopping. We don't have to count the beat or think hard about our next move. It just flows.

Thus, the church is a dance studio where people are invited in off the street. There are many times of sore muscles, sweaty bodies, and aching feet. But there are also moments of spinning and twirling and moving in harmony that are just plain fun. The church, thanks to the Spirit's rhythm and our Beloved partner, is moving us toward the dance of our lifetime. We anticipate a Day when we will execute every move without thinking or hesitation. We will simply be carried by the beat in our head and heart. And our eyes will not deviate from the eyes of our Beloved as he leads us. His love will flow to us and through us in uninterrupted measure (1 John 4:19).

Finally, I find it most revealing that James and Jude, the earthly brothers of Jesus, did not identify themselves as such in their New Testament letters. Instead, they both call themselves "servants of Jesus" (Jas 1:1; Jude 1:1). They no longer regarded Jesus or themselves from an earthly point of view. They recognized the larger family of which they were a member. They realized whom they danced around rather than who danced around them. And it changed their lives, both here and for eternity. The same can happen to us. The Spirit has been sent by the Beloved to make it so. And we are about to discover that the Spirit does much, much more than teach us to dance with our Beloved and with others.

QUESTIONS FOR DISCUSSION/REFLECTION:

1. How often do you meet with God's family? Is the gospel proclaimed clearly and often there?

2. What gifts are you able to share with other family members?

3. We bear with each other in Christian community. We bear with each other's oddities and idiosyncrasies, habits and quirks, pains and successes, even sins. What do others in your community bear patiently with you?

4. Thank God for the places of fellowship that you have enjoyed in your life. Pray for them and their progress in the faith right now.

5. Sing or listen to "For All the Saints."

Chapter 12: **We Need a Wedding Planner**

MANY ENGAGED COUPLES TODAY work with a wedding planner, also known as a wedding coordinator. The planner assumes the role similar to that of a stage manager in a theatre production. The planner takes care of all the details, large and small, behind the scenes to ensure that the production runs smoothly. The average wedding involves coordinating such things as the venue, guest seating, flowers, photographs/videos, attendants, families, food, music, dancing, introductions, speeches, tossing the garter, throwing the bouquet, cutting the cake, tossing the rice, etc. The role of the wedding planner is to allow the bride and groom to enjoy their moment on the wedding day with each other and family and friends without having to work or be distracted.

If you ever observe a wedding planner in action, you will notice that she is driven by a sense of timing. Everything happens on a schedule. As I write these words, my Bible is open on the desk before me. I can't help but marvel at how all of world history is on a schedule. We all know the universe is finely tuned, but world history is also finely timed. It begins with the careful numbering of the days of creation. Chapter 5 of Genesis gives us our first of several genealogies where we see when and how long people lived. Then we see forty days and nights of the great flood and a specific number of months and days Noah and his family are on the ark.

In between Genesis and Revelation, the Bible is full of thousands of numbers and dates. And everything happens at just the right time. After fourteen years, Joseph is released from prison just in time to prepare grain storage for a massive famine. Israel is captive in Egypt for over four hundred years, but then Pharoah ascends to power and Moses returns as a deliverer. Judges are raised at just the right time to deliver Israel. Later kings reign for a designated period. Indeed, "For everything there is a season, and a time for every matter under heaven: a time to be born and a time to die" (Eccl 3:1). You and I are part of this schedule. "In your book were written, every one of the days that were formed for me, when as yet there were none of them," Psalm 139:16 tells us. Every aspect of our Beloved's earthly existence was scheduled: "But when the fullness of time had come, God sent forth his Son, born of woman, born under the law, to redeem those who were under the law" (Gal 4:4–5).

Finally, fast forward through the end times of the New Testament to the last chapters of Revelation, where we see a bride adorned for her husband. Do you see in the metanarrative of the Bible what is happening on a huge scale for thousands of years? Do you see where it all ends? Do you see the dramatic, fantastic conclusion? All of world history, all of time, is moving toward our wedding day.

The wedding planner is orchestrating all of this. Every detail. And everything is right on schedule. In fact, a wedding planner is busiest right before the wedding. "And in the last days it shall be, God declares, that I will pour out my Spirit on all flesh, and your sons and daughters shall prophesy, and your young men shall see visions, and your old men shall dream dreams; even on my male servants and female servants in those days I will pour out my Spirit" (Acts 2:17–18).

Jesus told his disciples why he had to leave them in John 16:7, 11–15: "It is to your advantage that I go away, for if I do not go away, the Helper will not come to you. But if I go, I will send him to you . . . I still have many things to say to you, but you cannot bear them now. When the Spirit of truth comes, he will guide you into all the truth, for he will not speak on his own authority, but whatever he hears he will speak, and he will declare to you the things that are to come. He will glorify me, for he will take what is mine and declare it to you. All that the Father has is mine; therefore, I said that he will take what is mine and declare it to you."

"If I do not go away, the Helper will not come to you. But if I go, I will send him to you." Those words say it all. Our Helper is in each chapter of this book. Our Helper is working behind the scenes in our lives. The engagement period is really the work of the Holy Spirit. Without him, nothing is possible. He is preparing us for the big day. And he is tremendously busy taking care of every precise detail. So, let's review exactly what he does for Jesus and for us.

The Spirit guards and guarantees our salvation.	Eph 1:13; 4:30
The Spirit is the seal of our belonging to our Beloved.	2 Cor 1:21–22
The Spirit helps us communicate with our Beloved.	Jude 1:20; Rom 8:26–27
The Spirit regenerates and renews us.	Titus 3:5
The Spirit comforts us as we go through this hostile world.	1 Thess 1:6; 2 Cor 13:14
The Spirit fills us with joy so that we might abound with hope.	Rom 15:13
The Spirit leads us toward righteousness and away from the flesh.	Gal 5:16–18
The Spirit causes us to obey God's laws.	Ezek 36:27
The Spirit distributes gifts to us and for us.	1 Cor 12:4
The Spirit points us to Jesus.	John 15:26
The Spirit enables us to set our minds on things of him rather than on the flesh.	Rom 8:5
The Spirit pours God's love into us.	Rom 5:5
The Spirit gives life to us.	Rom 8:13–14
The Spirit washes, justifies, and sanctifies us.	1 Cor 6:11
The Spirit transforms us from one degree of glory to another.	2 Cor 3:17–18
The Spirit gives us love, joy, peace, patience, kindness, goodness, faithfulness, gentleness, self-control.	Gal 5:22–23
The Spirit inspired the 66 Love Letters and helps us understand and accept them.	2 Pet 1:21
The Spirit empowers us to say, "Jesus is Lord."	1 Cor 12:3
The Spirit gives us wisdom by which we can understand our Beloved.	1 Cor 2:12–13

The Holy Spirit puts us in the family of God and gives us gifts to build up the body of Christ (1 Cor 12:7). The body of believers is the perfect place to practice being married to our Beloved and to assure us that we are, in fact, connected to him. First John 3:21–24 tells us, "Beloved, if our heart does not condemn us, we have confidence before God; and whatever we ask we receive from him, because we keep his commandments and do what pleases him. And this is the commandment, that we believe in the name of his Son Jesus Christ and love one another, just as he has commanded us. Whoever keeps his commandments abides in God, and God in him. And by this we know that he abides in us, by the Spirit whom he has given us."

Our journey exploring this analogy of being engaged to Jesus began with his proposal and vow to us. The Spirit empowers us to understand and to accept this proposal. The Holy Spirit helps us see our need for wedding clothes and a makeover. The Holy Spirit gives us the clothing and the makeover. The Holy Spirit helps us detach from former lovers and attach to the Beloved. He removes our heart of stone and gives us a heart of flesh. He gives us a new spirit and himself to follow the Beloved's desires. The Holy Spirit gives us the three great gifts of faith, hope, and love. The Holy Spirit uses the registry of suffering to sustain us and transform us with his fruit so we can become one with our Beloved. The Holy Spirit instills faith and sustains it in us through the 66 Love Letters. The Holy Spirit moves us to submit to our Beloved's will and assures us of forgiveness when we fail and fall short of his glory. The Holy Spirit assimilates us into the family of God where we are loved and love. The Holy Spirit gives us the opportunities, courage, and words to speak that convey our Beloved to others. The Holy Spirit is also eager for our wedding with our Beloved. He prays for us with sighs and groans too deep for words (Rom 8:26).

As you can see, the Holy Spirit plays no small role in our engagement and preparation for our wedding. Without him, there is no engagement, no wedding, and no marriage for eternity. The Spirit's primary purpose is to magnify Jesus. He fixes our eyes on him. We have already covered one primary means he uses in our chapter on the 66 Love Letters. Now we come to the other primary means, the sacrament of holy communion. "Holy communion" summarizes the gospel—our engagement of grace— in a most delightful and tangible way.

Partaking of holy communion celebrates the two greatest events in history. It is a time for us to look back and remember that our Beloved paid the bride price and proposed to us at the cross. It is also a time for us to look forward to his return and remember that we will drink the cup of wine with him and thereby consummate our union with him. In this sacrament we see our Beloved's undivided devotion to us in his body and blood that thereby moves us toward undivided devotion to him.

Paul talks about our union with Jesus in 1 Corinthians 7:29–35: "This is what I mean, brothers: the appointed time has grown very short. From now on, let those who have wives live as though they had none, and those who mourn as though they were not mourning, and those who rejoice as though they were not rejoicing, and those who buy as though they had no goods, and those who deal with the world as though they had no dealings with it. For the present form of this world is passing away."

"I want you to be free from anxieties. The unmarried man is anxious about the things of the Lord, how to please the Lord. But the married man is anxious about worldly things, how to please his wife, and his interests are divided. And the unmarried or betrothed woman is anxious about the things of the Lord, how to be holy in body and spirit. But the married woman is anxious about worldly things, how to please her husband. I say this for your own benefit, not to lay any restraint upon you, but to promote good order and to secure your undivided devotion to the Lord."

In summary, the Holy Spirit is our comforter, counselor, helper, and intercessor. When we are tempted to fret, worry, and panic with all the preparation during our engagement, when we feel accused that we are just not good enough to get married to Jesus, it is the Spirit who reminds us of who our Beloved is, what he has done, and what he has promised. It is the Spirit who speaks to Jesus for us from the depth of our spirit and who speaks to us from the depth of Jesus' spirit (Rom 8:27).

The engagement period is a time to be endured. The Holy Spirit helps us endure by directing us to "run with perseverance the race that is set before us, looking to Jesus, the founder and perfecter of our faith, who for the joy that was set before him endured the cross, despising the shame, and is seated at the right hand of the throne of God" (Heb 12:1–2).

The 66 Love Letters refer to the Spirit as our seal and guarantee. He is the glue that keeps us connected to our Beloved. "It is God who establishes us with you in Christ, and has anointed us, and who has also put his seal on us and given us his Spirit in our hearts as a guarantee" (2 Cor 1:21–22).

It is tempting to drift into despair at various times in the engagement period. The world, our flesh, and satan attack us incessantly with doubts. "Have I done enough? Am I enough? I should be doing so much more. I have done so little. Will I be prepared when the time comes? Does God really love me? Does he forgive me for all my sins?" The calming influence of the Spirit points us to the truth. He reminds us of who and whose we are. We belong to our Beloved. We are his, and he is ours.

The Spirit reminds us what our Beloved is like. He is gentle and lowly. He is gracious and merciful. He abundantly pardons. He is unfailing and steadfast. He never leaves us or forsakes us. The Spirit keeps our minds in perfect peace by helping us focus not on ourselves but on our Beloved (Isa 26:3). He is enough and has given us all we need for life and godliness in himself (2 Pet 1:3).

Thanks to the Spirit's illuminating our hearts and minds and his now living inside us, we have a grasp of what our Beloved endured for us from the crib to the crypt in order to rescue us from eternal separation from him. Being overwhelmed by our unworthiness and by his great grace, we are now moved to become ecstatic and tell whoever will listen to us gush about the one who has chosen us, who has laid down his life for us, who is walking with us, who is planning to return for us, and who will take us to the wonderful home he is preparing for us. We simply cannot help ourselves. We must talk about Jesus.

QUESTIONS FOR DISCUSSION/REFLECTION:

1. What is the value of the Holy Spirit to you? What do you have because of him?

2. Read Galatians 5:22–23. Can you see how this fruit of the Spirit has increased in you throughout your life? Can you also see your need for more of it?

3. "The Spirit changes us by making Jesus wonderful to us." Has this been your experience? Do you have a sense of the perfect timing of the Spirit in your life, putting people and events in your path at the right moment, to move you toward your wedding day with Jesus?

4. How often do you participate in the Lord's Supper? What do you think about when you take it? Picture yourself dining with Jesus. What is that experience like for you?

5. Sing or listen to "Holy Spirit, Light Divine."

Chapter 13: **We Must Talk About Our Beloved**

IF YOU HAVE EVER known someone who is engaged, it is quite possible that they had one subject they liked to talk about more than any other—their intended spouse. Spouses are proud of their spouses. They like to introduce them to others. They like to sing their praises. And our Beloved is most worthy of conversation all the time. A question friends and family like to ask during the engagement is this: "How did you two meet?"

Those Hallmark movies must tap into something deep in our psyche. They definitely appeal to our quest for eternal love. But many of the storylines also begin with the two destined lovers as adversaries, even enemies. All stories in this fallen world present a conflict that must be resolved. And that is precisely the beginning we all have with Jesus. In our natural state, we want nothing to do with him. In fact, we hate him. Our default mode is anti-God. We don't trust him. We want our freedom and autonomy. We want to put ourselves in his place. We want to define "good" and "evil" for ourselves. And we most certainly do nothing to woo or win him to love us.

But then a most amazing thing happened. Our Beloved put himself in our place. He became human. He was born under the law. The spotless Lamb sacrificed his blood and life on the cross. He died the death we deserved. He paid the enormous debt we owed. Over time, after repeatedly hearing this good news, the Spirit opened our closed minds and softened our hard hearts. One day we found ourselves trusting him, loving him, and walking with him.

Our Beloved has given us one lasting image that captures his essence. It is the photograph we carry on our phone with us. It comes to us from the last of his love letters to us in Revelation 5:6. In heaven he is depicted as "a Lamb standing, as though it had been slain." He is standing next to his Father on the throne. Jesus gave this apocalypse, this unveiling of himself, to John the beloved disciple as he was imprisoned on Patmos and his congregation was being persecuted for refusing to bow down to the emperor and call him "Lord." That picture comforted and encouraged John's readers, and it does the same for us today as we persevere through the engagement period.

In that single image, we see that our Beloved is both all-loving and all-powerful. Scoffers in this world who don't know him like to attack one or the other of these qualities. But that final image encapsulates both with concise clarity. The slain lamb reminds us of his perfect obedience to the Father that led him to the cross to be sacrificed for us. He took the punishment we deserved. For God so loved the world. His standing next to the throne reminds us that the Father has given him all authority and power in heaven and on earth. Everything is under his control, despite appearances at times to the contrary. He is reigning from the throne now, today. All enemies—the world, sin, death, and satan—have been defeated. Read Revelation and you will discover that the battle of Armageddon is never fought. Jesus is not just *a* winner. He is *the* winner. That is our Beloved.

Upon his return to heaven after completing his rescue mission on earth, he was greeted by thousands and thousands of angels, saying with a loud voice, "Worthy is the Lamb who was slain, to receive power and wealth and wisdom and might and honor and glory and blessing!" (Rev 5:12). It was perfect seven-part praise. He is worthy of all our praise. That is our Beloved.

A local pastor likes to quip, "Unless we are talking about Jesus, we are off the subject."[1] There is indeed no greater subject for us to think about, write about, sing about, or talk about. Our Beloved is true, honorable, just, pure, lovely, commendable, excellent, worthy of praise (Phil 4:8). We are commanded in this passage to "think about these things." It is easy to think about one whom you love. We become obsessed. And why not?

1. Rev. Philip Cameron, pastor of Risen Savior in Broomfield, Colorado.

Our Beloved is patient and kind; he does not envy or boast; he is not arrogant or rude. He does not insist on his own way; he is not irritable or resentful; he does not rejoice at wrongdoing, but rejoices with the truth. He bears all things, believes all things, hopes all things, and endures all things.	1 Cor 13:4-7
Our Beloved sympathizes with our weaknesses because he has been tempted in every respect as we are.	Heb 4:15
Our Beloved is merciful and gracious, slow to anger and abounding in steadfast love and faithfulness, forgiving iniquity and transgression and sin, but who will by no means clear the guilty.	Exod 34:6-7
Our Beloved has borne our griefs and carried our sorrows; he was wounded for our transgressions; he was crushed for our iniquities; upon him was the chastisement that brought us peace and with his stripes we are healed.	Isa 53:4-5
Our Beloved remains faithful, even if we are faithless, for he cannot deny himself.	2 Tim 2:13
Our Beloved is gentle and lowly.	Matt 11:28
Our Beloved is a Wonderful Counselor, Mighty God, Everlasting Father, and Prince of Peace.	Isa 9:6

My beloved is radiant and ruddy, distinguished among ten thousand. His head is the finest gold; his locks are wavy, black as a raven. His eyes are like doves beside streams of water, bathed in milk, sitting beside a full pool. His cheeks are like beds of spices, mounds of sweet smelling herbs. His lips are lilies, dripping liquid myrrh. His arms are rods of gold, set with jewels, his body is polished ivory, bedecked with sapphires. His legs are alabaster columns, set on bases of gold. His appearance is like Lebanon, choice as the cedars. His mouth is most sweet, and he is altogether desirable. This is my beloved and this is my friend. (Song 5:10–16)

Our engagement, our salvation, is all about the praise, glory, and honor of Jesus. It is to him that praise, glory, and honor will resound for eternity for saving miserable wretches like us. Our story is much like *Beauty and the Beast*, and we are definitely not the beauty. He is. Now we are "a people for his own possession, that we may proclaim the excellencies of him who called us out of darkness into his marvelous light" (1 Pet 2:9). It is our greatest joy, honor, privilege, and pleasure to talk about our Beloved to others, to praise who he is, what he has done, and what he yet will do.

One word is used quite often in Scripture that describes relationships in this fallen world: *bearing*. Two people who have lived together for some time will be amazed at how much the other has put up with them. They know the other has borne with their moods, habits, weaknesses, and sins. I know there are people who have avoided me because it is too unpleasant for them to be around me. I know this to be true because there are people I have avoided because it was too unpleasant for me to be around them. This is not so with our Beloved. He bears all things about us. He endures all things about us. *All* things. Let that fact sink in.

He bears with our impatience and lack of kindness. He bears with our envying and boasting. He bears with our arrogance and rudeness. He bears with our insisting on our own way and when we are irritable and resentful. He bears with our doubts and fears. He bears with our sinfulness and sins. He bears with our weaknesses. He bears with our times of silence. He bears with our times of not listening to him or reading his 66 Love Letters. He bears with our avoiding being around his family. He bears with our tendency to focus more on things in this world than on our present or our future with him.

Therefore, it is only appropriate and fitting that we should boast about him.

"Let him who boasts boast in the Lord."	1 Cor 1:31
"'Let him who boasts boast of this, that he understands and knows Me, that I am the Lord who exercises lovingkindness, justice and righteousness on earth; for I delight in these things,' declares the Lord."	Jer 9:24
"But may it never be that I would boast except in the cross of our Lord Jesus Christ, through which the world has been crucified to me, and I to the world."	Gal 6:14
"So then let no one boast in men. For all things belong to you."	1 Cor 3:21
"My soul will make its boast in the Lord. The humble will hear it and rejoice."	Ps 34:2
"For by grace you have been saved through faith. And this is not your own doing; it is the gift of God, not a result of works, so that no one may boast."	Eph 2:8-9

I sometimes wonder if some in the church today have complicated evangelism and witnessing. We certainly can make it more about us than about him. Christian bookstores will offer many prescriptions as to how to best win converts to the faith. We have developed several methods in our attempts to reach people for Jesus, and we know apologetics inside and out to be able to debate anyone into the kingdom. But I wonder if in our quest to win converts we have relied too much on our reason and winsome approach. I wonder if we have focused more on our method than on our message.

Perhaps we should learn from Paul's attitude about Jesus:

"For I decided to know nothing among you except Jesus Christ and him crucified."	1 Cor 2:2
"Indeed, I count everything as loss because of the surpassing worth of knowing Christ Jesus my Lord."	Phil 3:8
"But I do not account my life of any value nor as precious to myself, if only I may finish my course and the ministry that I received from the Lord Jesus, to testify to the gospel of the grace of God."	Acts 20:24

The engagement period is a time to talk and think less about ourselves and to talk and think more about him. What does Jesus mean to you? Why is he important to you? Why do you believe in him? Why do you love him? Begin with what you know today. You will know him better five years from now. We start at different places and move at different rates. But at some level we know this: we were made to be with him. He is the peace, comfort, rest, satisfaction, acceptance, approval, thrill, pleasure, joy, assurance, security, meaning, significance, and unfailing, steadfast love we deeply, desperately desire.

In the last words Peter wrote, he urged his readers "to grow in the grace and knowledge of our Lord and Savior Jesus Christ" (2 Pet 3:18). *Grace* is "undeserved favor" and might be the second most prevalent word throughout the New Testament, surpassed not surprisingly by *love*. As the engagement time goes on, we will come to know ourselves and our Beloved better. We will see more of our sin and more of his grace. We will see that everything we have—every breath, every minute, every pleasure, every success—is undeserved favor from him. This will lead us to speak about him with humility and awe, with gratitude and love. There will be no need to argue or debate with another about him. For we will be telling our story with him. We will share what we have seen and what we have heard about him, and we will do so with gentleness and respect, for we honor him and we love him (1 Pet 3:15). He is our hope.

His grace might captivate others, too, so they will want to get to know him. When we share parts of his 66 Love Letters, others might be drawn as we have been. As 1 Corinthians 3:7 reminds us, "So neither he who plants nor he who waters is anything, but only God who gives the growth." His Word is much more powerful and effective than ours and "will not return empty, but it shall accomplish that which (He) purposes and shall succeed in the thing for which (He) sent it" (Isa 55:11). That is, after all, why we are with him. His Word touched our heart and mind, ignited faith in us, and drew us to him.

A word of caution needs to be given here, though: thinking and talking about Jesus will not only be exhilarating and exciting, but it will also increase our appetite to be with him. And that will lead us to long, groan, and anticipate as we await the wedding and marriage ahead. The world in its quest to make heaven on earth apart from God falsely believes that Christians should always feel good and be happy. But, as we are about to see, pining for our Beloved and our married life with him hurts.

QUESTIONS FOR DISCUSSION/REFLECTION:

1. Who in your life at present could benefit from hearing you talk about your experiences with Jesus?

2. What has kept you from witnessing more than you have? When you have witnessed, what fleshly motives or energy have you noticed? How have you relied on God in those times?

3. List all the planters and waterers of faith in your life. Include pastors, Sunday school teachers, youth workers, family, friends, and authors. Why did you listen to them? Thank God for moving through them.

4. Read 1 Peter 2:9. What "excellencies" of your Beloved are you most eager to share with others?

5. Sing or listen to "All Hail the Power of Jesus' Name."

Chapter 14: **We Long, Groan, and Anticipate**

I THINK IT HELPS, from time to time, to remember this truth: we all want something right now that we can't fully have yet. Pause and think about that. I want the problem-free church right now, the problem-free country right now, the problem-free world right now. I want to feel so close to God right now. I want to feel so close to family and friends right now. I want to be the man I should be, the teacher I should be, the friend I should be. I want to be the Christian I should be right now. "I do not do what I want, but I do the very thing I hate" (Rom 7:15). Welcome to being engaged. We aren't yet wearing our wedding clothes. Our makeover is not yet complete. We still see unsightly blemishes in the mirror daily and drag around a body of death (Rom 7:24). And, most of all, we do not see our Beloved's face yet.

Sometimes we fight against this reality by trying to force our feelings to the contrary. Sometimes we think we know more than we really know. Sometimes we deceive ourselves to believe we act better than we do and for purer motives than we really have. Sometimes we manufacture feelings of ecstasy in hopes they will last. We want so desperately to be home with our Lord. We long for shalom, the restoration of all creation to the condition in which it was intended to be. God has, after all, "put eternity into man's heart" (Eccl 3:11).

There is a word that is sprinkled throughout Scripture that describes our present condition and position rather well—*groaning*. I think it is the ultimate homesickness. Larry Crabb puts it well in *Inside Out*: "The longings of our heart must be faced. The disappointment of our soul must be experienced. Only then will we learn to pant after God in eager anticipation of his coming, when every desire will be satisfied."[1] How disappointed are you with life in this world?

After my last divorce, I desperately longed to hear from my ex-wife. Like the father of the prodigal son, I ached and yearned for her to return. After a few years, I finally realized that underneath that longing was a deeper one: I was actually longing for Jesus to return for me. In the deeper part of my redeemed heart, I really wanted the greater love more than I wanted the lesser love.

I have two indelible memories etched in my mind as I write this chapter.

The first one comes from my dear aunt, who died of stage four bone marrow cancer after living the last two years of her life with it. I had the privilege and honor of witnessing this holy time in her life. My last memory of her is watching my uncle and my mother care for her at her home in Lakewood, Colorado. They took turns wiping her face with a cool cloth and putting drops of morphine on her tongue to ease her pain. My cousin and I took turns reading Psalms aloud. On my last visit prior to her departing to be with the Lord, she was lying on her back, apparently sleeping, when suddenly she sprang upright and declared with energetic urgency, "I want to see God." Then she lay back down and closed her eyes.

The second memory is what my mother insisted the last several years before the Lord called her home. She refused to say "goodbye." She declared that we should conclude every visit and every phone call with "see you later" rather than "goodbye." And she would correct us if we misspoke. I think she was longing, groaning, and anticipating.

If I could condense my spiritual journey, my sanctification, it would be this way. Like these two dear female relatives, I have a heightened longing to be with God. By God's grace, God's chosen get to the place where David was in Psalm 73:25: "Whom have I in heaven but you? And there is nothing on earth that I desire besides you. My flesh and my heart may fail, but God is the strength of my heart and my portion forever." We get to the place where Paul was in Philippians 1:22–23: "If I am to live in the flesh, that means fruitful labor for me. Yet which I shall choose I cannot tell. I am hard pressed between the two. My desire is to depart and be with Christ, for that is far better."

To some people such thinking appears fatalistic or depressing. It appears to be ungrateful for the gifts and purposes of God in this world.

1. Crabb, *Inside Out*, 96.

But think about it. The best family points us to the family of God. But so does the worst family. The best marriage points us to God, but so does the worst one. Everything in this world directs our attention and affections toward him. Pleasures and joys of this world are fleeting and momentary. They don't last or fully satisfy. The designer never meant for them to do so. To paraphrase Colossians 1:13-20, everything was made by, for, and through Jesus so that in him he might have the supremacy. Jesus says in Revelation 22:13, "I am the Alpha and the Omega, the first and the last, the beginning and the end."

Philippians 3:10–14, 20–21 gives us the mindset to have as we prepare for our eternal union with our Beloved:

> "That I may know him and the power of his resurrection, and may share his sufferings, becoming like him in his death, that by any means possible I may attain the resurrection from the dead. Not that I have already obtained this or am already perfect, but I press on to make it my own, because Christ Jesus has made me his own. Brothers, I do not consider that I have made it my own. But one thing I do: forgetting what lies behind and straining forward to what lies ahead, I press on toward the goal for the prize of the upward call of God in Christ Jesus . . . our citizenship is in heaven, and from it we await a Savior, the Lord Jesus Christ, who will transform our lowly body to be like his glorious body."

"Our citizenship is in heaven." That means we are strangers and foreigners here. We will feel out of place and restless. During this engagement period—also known as the church age, the thousand-year-reign of Christ, or the tribulation—we strain against our sinful nature, the world, and the devil. Those three forces tempt us to make this world our home. But our soul is at peace under the promises and grace of the Beloved, so we are strengthened and preserved by looking forward to the life to come. We move gradually toward having undivided devotion to our Beloved. That entails daily repentance.

I have heard that *repentance* essentially means "to turn" or "to change the mind." Luther's first thesis of his famous *Ninety-five Theses* is maintaining that the entire life of the Christian is one of continual (as in nonstop) repentance. I find it helpful to recall the story of Lot and his wife leaving Sodom and Gomorrah. They were instructed by the two angels not to look back as they left the two depraved cities (Gen 19). It is a good visual for the present stage we are in of leaving this world and moving toward home and being with our Beloved. Don't look back.

We need to turn away from whatever we have clung to here and turn toward clinging to the one who is our very life. So, we repent, we turn away from trusting in our own righteousness and turn toward trusting in the righteousness of Jesus to make us right with God and worthy of entrance to our eternal home. Our Lord urged his people in the seven letters to churches in Revelation chapters 2 and 3 to repent of, to turn away from, sexual immorality, idolatry, and false teaching. John mentions the three big allures of the world in 1 John 2:16–17 that we should not love—pride, greed, and lust—because "the world is passing away along with its desires." Indeed, the entire world will one day pass away with fire and brimstone just as Sodom and Gomorrah did. Luther said, "We should learn to bring our eyes, our hearts, and souls to bear upon yonder life in heaven and in a lively hope await it with joy. For if we would be Christians, the ultimate objects of our quest should not be marrying, giving in marriage, buying, selling, planting, building . . . But our ultimate quest should be something better and higher: the blessed inheritance in heaven that does not pass away."[2]

At the end of the movie *Jerry Maguire*, Jerry says one of his most memorable lines to his sweetheart: "You complete me." I think that summarizes our feelings of this engagement period well. We feel incomplete because we are. Ever since Adam and Eve rebelliously separated themselves from God and tried to find their fulfillment and well-being in their own understanding of good and evil, we have been incomplete. We are not whole. We are broken and fragmented. We are missing something or, to be more precise, someone. So, we groan and ache for our Beloved, to simply be in his presence and to gaze upon his beauty as David longed to be (Ps 27:4). But we will not be complete, we will not be fulfilled, we will not be whole, until we are totally, completely with him and rid of our present sinful flesh.

This is the most painful part of our engagement. We desperately long to be satisfied. It hurts. It is agony. We try to deaden the pain by drinking from leaky wells. We hope this meal, that sexual experience, a spouse, children, career, appearance, house, trip, possession, exercise, busyness, or whatever will take away the pain. It provides relief for only a very brief moment, seconds at best in the grand scheme of things. And then the ache returns to our consciousness, until we try to numb it again with our chosen narcotic.

2. Plass, *What Luther Says Vol. II*, 619.

Dane Ortlund writes of this groaning in his book *Deeper*: "For we know that the whole creation has been groaning together in the pains of childbirth until now. 'The whole creation' (Rom 8:22) does not mean the natural created order minus humans. We are included in that futility. We, too, groan inwardly as we wait eagerly for God to put all things right in the end."[3] Ortlund then provides this positive perspective of our groaning: "The struggle itself reflects life. If we were not regenerate, we simply wouldn't care. The longing for Jesus, the frustration at our falls, the desire to be fully yielded to God—these are the cries of life, even if immature life."[4] It is good that we groan for what we are not yet fully experiencing.

Our longing for ultimate satisfaction beckons us to increasingly look to Jesus. He becomes more beautiful and attractive to our heart daily. The engagement period is a time to get to know each other better. Our Beloved shows that he knows us most intimately. He counts the times we toss and turn in our sleep; he gathers our tears in a bottle (Ps 56:8); he knows the number of hairs on our head (Luke 12:7); he knows a word before it is on our tongue (Ps 139:4). But our knowledge of Jesus and his grace has been stunted and blunted by distractions in this world and by our stubborn, self-absorbed flesh.

Ortlund gives this concluding advice at the end of his book, "It is one thing to believe the gospel with our minds, and another to work it deep into our hearts. The final conclusion, the deepest secret, to growing in Christ is this: look to him. Set your gaze upon him. Abide in him, hour by hour. Draw strength from his love."[5] He is echoing Paul's words to us in 2 Corinthians 4:18: "As we look not to the things that are seen but to the things that are unseen. For the things that are seen are transient, but the things that are unseen are eternal."

There is another theme running throughout God's Word: there is only one thing we need and, thanks be to God, we have him (Luke 10:38–42)! As Tim Keller writes, "We don't realize Jesus is all we need until Jesus is all we have."[6] That will most certainly be the case on our deathbed, but it is also the case in each and every minute today. I need him to give me my next breath. I need him to help me get back to sleep most nights. I need him to enable me to get out of bed every day. I need him to do whatever good he

3. Ortlund, *Deeper*, 141.

4. Ortlund, *Deeper*, 141.

5. Ortlund, *Deeper*, 171.

6. Keller, *Counterfeit Gods*, 20.

will do through me in this world. I need him to forgive me yet again. I need him to get me safely home by his side. I need him.

David knew this as revealed in Psalms 62 and 63. "For God alone my soul waits in silence; from him comes my salvation, my fortress; I shall not be greatly shaken" (Ps 62:1–2). "O God, you are my God; earnestly I seek you; my soul thirsts for you; my flesh faints for you, as in a dry and weary land where there is no water. So I have looked upon you in the sanctuary, beholding your power and glory. Because your steadfast love is better than life, my lips will praise you" (Ps 63:1–3). I need him.

The engagement period can thus feel excruciatingly lonely. As Larry Crabb has written in his best seller *Inside Out*, "What we want is simply not available, not until heaven. The more aware we become of our most passionate longings, the more lonely and sad we feel."[7] We thirst to see God and be with him. This thirst increases as he sanctifies us. How fitting it is that our Beloved writes this in the last few words in the last chapter of the last love letter he wrote us, "The Spirit and the Bride say, 'Come.' And let the one who hears say, 'Come.' And let the one who is thirsty come; let the one who desires take the water of life without price" (Rev 22:17).

Instead of quenching our thirst, this engagement time seems only to heighten it. The whole of the Christian life is the present possession of inherited blessings, which will be realized in fuller measure in the life to come. The longing, groaning, and anticipating of such experience will come to an end when our Beloved returns for us. The engagement period will stop, and the marriage of all marriages will begin. And we will thirst no more, for we will be with him in the flesh. The best is yet to come.

QUESTIONS FOR DISCUSSION/REFLECTION:

1. What does your flesh use as a narcotic to numb the groaning and aching for shalom?

2. How much of your time do you spend looking back at your life in this world? How much of your time do you spend looking forward to life in the next world? What are the effects of dwelling on those two perspectives?

7. Crabb, *Inside Out*, 71.

3. "We don't realize Jesus is all we need until Jesus is all we have." Have you experienced this? If "yes," what were the circumstances? Thank him now for being your all in all.

4. How often do you feel lonely in this world? What do you groan and long for? Read Matthew 5:4.

5. Sing or listen to "Abide With Me."

Chapter 15: **We Cleave and Become One Flesh**

ONENESS. UNITY. PRESENCE. SHALOM. These are the deepest desires of our redeemed heart. This is what lies ahead of us with our Beloved. We catch glimpses of them now as we remember our baptism, as we take communion, as we read the Word, as we pray, as we worship, and as we fellowship with other believers. But an entirely new and glorious experience awaits us when we are taken home. It will be the most intensely pleasurable experience we have ever had.

In John 17:20–21, 24, Jesus prays a most profound and intimate request of our Father: "I do not ask for these only, but also for those who will believe in me through their word, that they may all be one, just as you, Father, are in me, and I in you, that they also may be in us, so that the world may believe that you have sent me . . . Father, I desire that they also, whom you have given me, may be with me where I am, to see my glory that you have given me because you loved me before the foundation of the world."

The most frequent description of believers in the New Testament is our being "in Christ" and "Christ in us." This is the most poignant and mysterious aspect of our "now-but-not-yet" engagement experience. We are now, today, one with our Beloved. We are one with his family. There are about 128 verses in the New Testament that talk directly about our being in Christ. Look at what is ours thanks to our being in our Beloved:

peace with God	Rom 5:1	righteous	Rom 5:19
dead to sin	Rom 6:11	alive to God	Rom 6:11
under grace	Rom 6:14	bearing fruit	Rom 7:4
not condemned	Rom 8:1	led by the Spirit	Rom 8:14
the mind of Christ	I Cor 2:16	the Spirit's temple	I Cor 3:16
sanctified, justified	I Cor 6:11	able to comfort others	2 Cor 1:4
transformed	2 Cor 3:18	inwardly renewed	2 Cor 4:16
living for him	2 Cor 5:15	a new creation	2 Cor 5:17
his ambassadors	2 Cor 5:20	not under the law	Gal 3:25
forgiven	Eph 1:7	seated with Christ	Eph 2:6
do good works	Eph 2:10	may approach God	Eph 3:12
holy, without blemish	Col 1:22	destined for paradise	Col 3:4
have what we need	2 Pet 1:3	have an advocate	1 John 2:1
dearly loved	1 John 3:1	have eternal life	1 John 5:13

It is a good time to recall that our Lord's first miracle was turning water into wine at a wedding feast (John 2:11). It was foreshadowing the eternal feast to come. Our engagement period will culminate when our Beloved returns for us, and we will cleave and become one with him. At that point we will have a wedding celebration, consummate our eternal relationship with him by drinking wine together, and move into the home of righteousness he has prepared for us. We will live happily ever after with our true soulmate.

I have had several friends over the years express disappointment that they will not remain married to their earthly spouse in the new heavens and new earth (Matt 22:30). I think that they do not fully realize what will replace it. It is not earthly marriage or parenthood that ultimately defines or fulfills us. It is God and our relationship with him. We will be completely satisfied in him. We were created to be one with him.

When I graduated from high school, I had one goal for life: to marry a Christian woman and have a loving, Christian family. In retrospect, it was not a bad desire, but it should not have been an ultimate goal for a disciple of Jesus. It was an idol. But now, fifty years later, I see that God has, in fact, granted me that desire out of pure grace. I am engaged to the spouse of my dreams who can totally fulfill me and forever forgive me. And he has planted me in a huge, loving Christian family. I have brothers and sisters from every nation and language (Dan 7:14)! This is beyond what I asked or imagined as an eighteen-year-old product of a divorced, alcoholic home. And this marriage and family will never end! In addition, these relationships will be characterized by endless love. No more tears or mourning from divisions and separations.

God—the eternal, perfect, pure, all-knowing, and all-powerful being—marries us, the temporal, imperfect, rebellious, impotent creatures that we are, in this tent. "He who is joined to the Lord becomes one spirit with him" (1 Cor 6:17). Earthly marriage is sacred and beautiful because it is the dress rehearsal, the foreshadowing, of the ultimate sacred and beautiful marriage of God and us. And our Beloved will rightly receive all the accolades from heaven and earth for his great love, mercy, and grace in his choosing and enacting the rescue and renewal of us.

> Blessed be the God and Father of our Lord Jesus Christ! According to his great mercy, he has caused us to be born again to a living hope through the resurrection of Jesus Christ from the dead, to an inheritance that is imperishable, undefiled, and unfading, kept in heaven for you, who by God's power are being guarded through faith for a salvation ready to be revealed in the last time. In this you rejoice, though now for a little while, if necessary, you have been grieved by various trials, so that the tested genuineness of your faith—more precious than gold that perishes though it is tested by fire—may be found to result in praise and glory and honor at the revelation of Jesus Christ. (1 Pet 1:3–7)

One of the most powerful longings in the human heart is for unity. We hate divorce, firings, divisions, and rejections. Becoming one flesh is about knowing—truly, deeply knowing another—and being committed to each other. It is walking in step together. God exists as an eternally unified diversity in the community of the Trinity. His love and grace invite us and pave the way for us to join in that holy community that is characterized by willful, cheerful giving, not by coercing or manipulating. Ephesians 4:13 tells us that this is why God gave the Church various gifts, "until we all attain to the unity of the faith and of the knowledge of the Son of God, to mature manhood, to the measure of the stature of the fullness of Christ."

John 17:3 tells us, "And this is eternal life, that they know you the only true God, and Jesus Christ whom you have sent." First Corinthians

13:12 tells us, "For now we see in a mirror dimly, but then face to face. Now I know in part; then I shall know fully, even as I have been fully known." Paul's, and our, ultimate goal is that we "may know him and the power of his resurrection" (Phil 3:10). We will have direct, personal experience with God! We will see him and be in his holy presence! This engagement time is temporary; it will end. But the marriage time will be eternal; it will never end.

Psalm 116:15 tells us that the death of his saints is precious to God. Why is that? Because he longs to be with us. He longs for us to be with him. He longs for our address to change from this temporal, broken world to his restored, perfect home. Psalm 16:10–11 tells us, "For you will not abandon my soul to Sheol, or let your holy one see corruption. You make known to me the path of life; in your presence there is fullness of joy; at your right hand are pleasures forevermore."

I have always marveled at believers who have endured tremendous trials. Job lost all ten of his children in a horrific accident. His vast wealth was stolen by evil marauders. And his robust health deteriorated to where he had painful sores all over his body. As if these horrific trials were not enough, his wife, partner, and companion no longer walked equally yoked with him. In her anger toward God for their calamities, she wanted her husband to curse God and die (Job 2:9). What would move such a beleaguered man to get out of bed each day and go on living?

The answer is found in Job's confession in Job 19:25–26: "I know that my Redeemer lives, and at the last he will stand upon the earth. And after my skin has been thus destroyed, yet in my flesh I shall see God." Job, like all believers, was trusting that God had bought him back from bondage to sin, death, and the devil. He was banking his future eternal security on the fact that God would raise him from the dead and that Job would see the face of God. Naked and empty-handed, he had come from God, and naked and empty-handed he would return to him (Job 1:21). And let's not forget what quieted Job's questioning of his trials and tribulations in this world: "I had heard of you by the hearing of the ear, but now my eye sees you; therefore, I despise myself and repent in dust and ashes" (Job 42:5–6).

Presence. The resurrection of our Beloved changes everything. Ponder Paul's words to the Corinthians: "He who raised the Lord Jesus will raise us also with Jesus and bring us with you into his presence" (2 Cor 4:14). You will be raised from the dead and ushered into an eternity of happily ever after. Paul David Tripp says it well in his rich devotional *New Morning Mercies*:

"He will satisfy your heart as nothing else can. You were made for him. Your heart was designed to be controlled by worship of him. Your inner security is meant to come from rest in him . . . God is the peace that you're looking for. He is the satisfaction that your heart seeks. He is the rest that you crave, the joy you long for, and the comfort your heart desires."[1]

I find it fascinating that the Jews would read Song of Solomon aloud on the last day of Passover. They knew God was their husband. They knew he had chosen them to be his people. Revelation 22:3–5 tells us, "No longer will there be anything accursed, but the throne of God and of the Lamb will be in it, and his servants will worship him. They will see his face, and his name will be on their foreheads. And night will be no more. They will need no light or lamp or sun, for the Lord God will be their light, and they will reign forever and ever."

Revelation 21:27 reveals to us that "nothing unclean will ever enter it, nor anyone who does what is detestable or false, but only those who are written in the Lamb's book of life." There will be no satan to tempt us! There will be no self-absorbed flesh clinging to us! There will be no fallen world to vex us! The fullness of what Jesus purchased for us will be given to us: full freedom from every sinful thing that hinders our enjoyment and worship of God. Our new and glorified body will join our soul at the resurrection, and we will be fully equipped to live in the land of righteousness with our Beloved and his family. We will at last be able to fully experience the glory of oneness, unity, and presence with him.

In the Old Testament, the temple was God's residence among his people. But in the new earth, there is no temple. There is no need as each believer is the temple of the Holy Spirit, where God resides. You cannot get more intimate than being inside another. Ephesians chapter 2, that rich chapter along with Ephesians 1 that is essentially the summary of this entire book, concludes with these words: "You are fellow citizens with the saints and members of the household of God, built on the foundation of the apostles and prophets, Christ Jesus himself being the cornerstone, in whom the whole structure, being joined together, grows into a holy temple in the Lord. In him you also are being built together into a dwelling place for God by the Spirit" (Eph 2:19–22). Our unity with our Beloved unites us with all his people. "But now in Christ Jesus you who once were far off have been brought near by the blood of Christ . . . that he might create in himself one new man in place of the two" (Eph 2:13, 15).

1. Tripp, *New Morning Mercies*, May 24.

The best word to describe the consummation and new home with our Beloved is *shalom*. It embodies more than what we think of in the word *peace*. It is unity and harmony. It is wholeness, completion, satisfaction, fulfillment. We will hunger for nothing when we have shalom because we will have everything. Shalom will be the restored state of all creation before the fall. Every miracle Jesus performed was a sign that indeed the kingdom of God had come in him. In the kingdom of God the blind see, the lame walk, the deaf hear, the dead are alive. No wonder why several parables tell us life with our Beloved is worth more than the sum of all our earthly possessions (Matt 13:44–46).

We will have shalom when we will finally see and be with our Beloved. We will have a new and glorified body. We will have eternal rest from fighting against sin, satan, and the fallen curse in the world. Gone will be any striving for identity, meaning, or fulfillment in some created thing in this world. Here in the engagement period our feelings are fickle; they rise and fall. Our understanding is incomplete; we have questions and doubts. Our actions are erratic; we disobey and fall. We are consistently inconsistent! But there in the eternal marriage we will at last be totally complete, whole, and in harmony with ourselves, with others, with nature, and with God. We will always function according to God's design for us. Life will be perfect.

There is a biblical truth rarely heard in many churches these days and it is this. In whose image were you born? Many people will respond with "God's," but Genesis 5:1b—3 tells us, "When God created man, he made him in the likeness of God. Male and female he created them, and he blessed them and named them Man when they were created. When Adam had lived 130 years, he fathered a son in his own likeness, after his image, and named him Seth." And what is Adam's image like? It is selfish, idolatrous, and it ends in death. It relies on his own understanding of good and evil rather than on God's.

Have you noticed how many spouses, after being together for many years, seem to resemble each other? In fact, when two become one, people now think of the two as one. Where the husband goes, his wife is with him, even if she isn't there physically. When we believe our Beloved's proposal for lifelong union is for us and that he has done all that is necessary to make it so, our oneness begins. We even take his name as we are then called "Christian." First Corinthians 15:49 tells us, "Just as we have borne the image of the man of dust, we shall also bear the image of the man of heaven." And just as an earthly couple gradually resemble each other more and more, so too are we "being transformed into the same image from one degree of glory to another" (2 Cor 3:18).

And the exciting thing for us to anticipate is this: we are predestined to become like Jesus. That challenging but comforting concept bookends our relationship with God. Our Beloved chose us or predestined us to be his before creation (Eph 1:4). But in the end, when all is made new, he has predestined us to be conformed to the image of Jesus. Listen to the absolute certainty of this in Romans 8:29–30: "For those whom he foreknew he also predestined to be conformed to the image of his Son . . . And those whom he predestined he also called, and those whom he called he also justified, and those whom he justified he also glorified." "Glorified" is in the past tense, as though it is already finished. Paul speaks with the same certainty to the believers at Philippi: "And I am sure of this, that he who began a good work in you will bring it to completion at the day of Jesus Christ" (Phil 1:6). That good work is becoming like our Beloved, becoming fully restored in his image.

Our faith journey during this engagement time, therefore, is really a journey into Jesus himself. Dane Ortlund says in *Deeper*, "The Christian life is at heart not a matter of doing more or behaving better but of going deeper. We grow specifically by going deeper into the gospel, into the love of Christ and our experienced union with Him."[2] As Colossians 1:16 essentially says, "All things in heaven and on earth were created by, for, and through him." Later in Colossians 3:3 Paul says, "For you have died, and your life is hidden with Christ in God. When Christ who is your life appears, then you also will appear with him in glory."

In his book *Ephesians* Darrell Johnson says, "Even now we share in Jesus' new order, in Jesus' victory, in Jesus' dominion . . . We have been transferred into the new order of life, even while still in the old."[3] God has made us alive with Christ; he has raised us up with Christ; he has seated us with him on the throne (Eph 2:5–6). We are betrothed to our Beloved. We are legally married now. "We are a new creation. The old has passed away; the new has come. All this is from God" (2 Cor 5:17–18).

The implications of the above are tremendously and deeply profound. The overarching storyline of the Bible and therefore all of life in this world is this: creation, fall, redemption, restoration. God made us to be with him; we rebelled and became separated from him; God came into our fallen

2. Ortlund, *Deeper*, 153.

3. Johnson, *Ephesians*, 130–131.

world, rescued us, and reunited us with him; now God is restoring all creation and all believers to return to his original design of being together in harmony. Everything that has transpired in your life and mine makes sense only in relation to this metanarrative. The cleaving and becoming one flesh with our Beloved has already begun! But it won't be complete until he returns for us. The Trinity is moving in, around, and through us now. Here and now, we stumble and fall in our polluted, lawless, demanding flesh. But there and then, we will dance flawlessly in perfect rhythm in our white robes of righteousness with our Beloved.

For now, our redeemed hearts long for our Beloved's life to increase in ours and for our fleshly life to decrease. "I have been crucified with Christ. It is no longer I who live, but Christ who lives in me. And the life I now live in the flesh I lived by faith in the Son of God, who loved me and gave himself for me" (Gal 2:20). Indeed, anything good proceeding from us is literally coming from Jesus himself in us.

First John 3:2–3 says, "Beloved, we are God's children now, and what we will be has not yet appeared; but we know that when he appears we shall be like him, because we shall see him as he is. And everyone who thus hopes in him purifies himself as he is pure." To be like our Beloved, to be with our Beloved: this is the desire of every bride's heart.

Paul writes about our ultimate restoration beautifully in 1 Corinthians 15:42–49:

> So is it with the resurrection of the dead. What is sown is perishable; what is raised is imperishable. It is sown in dishonor; it is raised in glory. It is sown in weakness; it is raised in power. It is sown a natural body; it is raised a spiritual body. If there is a natural body, there is also a spiritual body. Thus, it is written, "The first man Adam became a living being"; the last Adam became a life-giving spirit. But it is not the spiritual that is first but the natural, then the spiritual. The first man was from the earth, a man of dust, so also are those who are of the dust; the second man is from heaven. As was the man of dust, so also are those who are of the dust, and as is the man of heaven, so also are those who are of heaven. Just as we have borne the image of the man of dust, we shall also bear the image of the man of heaven.

We pray Psalm 17:8, 15: "Keep me as the apple of your eye; hide me in the shadow of your wings . . . As for me, I shall behold your face in righteousness; when I awake, I shall be satisfied with your likeness." In Revelation 21:6 Jesus says, "It is done!" The last time Jesus said those words was at the cross when he referred to his completing our redemption and justification. The next time Jesus will say those words will be at his return, when he will complete our restoration and sanctification.

Think of it: our Beloved was raised from the dead by our Father. He was given all power and authority in heaven and earth. He rescued us from being dead in sin and captive to evil and made us alive with him, raised us up with him, seated us with him in heaven, and now lives in us and through us. Listen to his heart at the end of his high-priestly prayer the night before he died: "I in them and you in me, that they may become perfectly one, so that the world may know that you sent me and loved them even as you loved me. Father, I desire that they also, whom you have given me, may be with me where I am, to see my glory that you have given me because you loved me before the foundation of the world" (John 17:23–24).

Our Beloved gives us a wonderful description of our new home with him in Revelation 21:4: "He will wipe away every tear from their eyes, and death shall be no more, neither shall there be mourning, nor crying, nor pain anymore, for the former things have passed away." "No longer will there be anything accursed, but the throne of God and of the Lamb will be in it" (Rev 22:3).

Three times our Beloved says reassuringly to us in his last chapter of his last love letter to us, "Behold, I am coming soon" (Rev 22:7, 12, 20). Our wedding day is coming! What a joyous day it will be when our engagement ends and our marriage begins. All the preparing, longing, aching, and waiting will be over. At last, we will be without sin, and we will be with our Beloved, and we will see his face (Rev 22:4)!

"The Spirit and the Bride say, 'Come.' And let the one who hears say, 'Come.' And let the one who is thirsty come; let the one who desires take the water of life without price" (Rev 22:17).

"'Surely, I am coming soon.' Amen. Come, Lord Jesus!" (Rev 22:20).

QUESTIONS FOR DISCUSSION/REFLECTION:

1. Which qualities of being "in Christ" listed at the beginning of this chapter are most joyous for you? Which qualities are hardest for you to believe are true?

2. Can you see how God has used everything in your life to either redeem you to him or to restore you to being like him?

3. We have already been made alive, been raised, and been seated with him in the heavenly places (Eph 2:3–4). Galatians speaks to our being adopted as sons. *We Are Engaged!* speaks to our being married to Jesus. List all the rich blessings in Christ these analogies help you understand about your relationship with him.

4. Read Ephesians chapters 1 and 2. Meditate on what your Beloved has done, is doing, and will do for you. Thank and praise him now.

5. Sing or listen to "How Great Thou Art."

Bibliography

Amazing Hymns. "Come Thou Fount of Every Blessing." https://amazinghymns.com/come-thou-fount-of-every-blessing/.

Bonhoeffer, Dietrich. *The Cost of Discipleship*. New York: Touchstone, 1959.

Crabb, Larry. *Inside Out*. Colorado Springs, CO: Navpress, 1988.

Johnson, Darrell. *Ephesians*. Vancouver: Pastorate, 2022.

Keller, Timothy. *Counterfeit Gods*. New York: Penguin, 2009.

———. *The Reason for God*. New York: Penguin, 2008.

———. "Uncovering Hope." OICCU, Feb. 23, 2015. YouTube video, 1:00:50.

Lewis, C. S. *The Collected Letters of C. S. Lewis*. San Francisco: Harper, 2004.

———. *Mere Christianity*. New York: HarperOne, 1980.

The Lutheran Hymnal. St. Louis: Concordia, 1941.

The Lutheran Study Bible (ESV). St. Louis: Concordia, 2009.

Luther, Martin. "Commentary on Galatians, Chapters 5–6." In *Luther's Works*, Vol. 27, edited by Jaroslav Pelikan. St. Louis: Concordia, 1992.

Moulds, Russ. "Key Reformation Themes: A Summary." https://wp.cune.edu/twokingdoms2/files/2016/12/Key-Reformation-Themes-a-Summary.pdf.

King, Martin Luther, Jr. "Dr. Martin Luther King, Jr.'s 1962 Speech in NYC." New York State Museum, Jan. 20, 2014. YouTube video, 26:34.

Ortlund, Dane. *Deeper*. Wheaton, IL: Crossway, 2021.

———. *Gentle and Lowly*. Wheaton, IL: Crossway, 2020.

Plass, Ewald M. *What Luther Says, Vol. II*. St. Louis: Concordia, 1959.

Tripp, Paul David. *New Morning Mercies*. Wheaton, IL: Crossway, 2014.